Véronique Tadjo is the leading African Francophone woman writer of her generation. Tadjo is a novelist, poet, writer of children's books and travel literature. She is also a painter and illustrator. Born of an Ivorian father and a French mother in Paris, she was brought up in Abidjan. She has a doctorate in African American Studies and has traveled extensively in West Africa, Europe, USA and Latin America. She taught at the University of Abidjan for several years and has conducted many workshops on writing (and book illustration for children) in numerous countries. She has published several books and her novel *Reine Pokou* (Queen Pokou) was awarded the prestigious literary prize "Grand Prix Littéraire d'Afrique Noire" in 2005. She has been facilitating writing workshops for the Caine Prize for African Writing for several years. Tadjo currently lives in South Africa where she is Head of French Studies in the School of Literature & Language Studies, University of Witwatersrand in Johannesburg.

About the Translator

Janis A. Mayes is a professor of African/Diasporan Literatures and Cultural Studies in the Department of African American Studies at Syracuse University, USA. Her areas of specialization involve African and Caribbean literatures in French and English languages; Black women's international writing and Translation Studies. A literary translator, her scholarship includes: *The City Where No One Dies*, translated from the French, *La ville où nul ne meurt* by Bernard Dadié; *Mapping Intersections: African Literature and Africa's Development* (edited with Anne V. Adams); *Une pluie de mots: Anthologie bilingue de la poésie féminine en Afrique francophone/ A Rain of Words: Bilingual Anthology of Women's Poetry in Francophone Africa* (editor, Irène Assiba d"Almeida, forthcoming University of Virginia Press, 2008). A Fulbright scholar, Mayes has taught at the Université Nationale de Côte d'Ivoire (Abidjan) and Cheikh Anta Diop Université (Dakar). She is founding director of the SU/AAS study abroad program: *Paris Noir: Literature, Art and Contemporary Life in Diaspora*. Mayes is also past President of the African Literature Association (ALA).

The Blind Kingdom

Véronique Tadjo

Translated from the French by Janis A. Mayes

ayebia

An Adinkra symbol meaning
Ntesie maternasie
A symbol of knowledge and wisdom

Copyright © 2008 Véronique Tadjo
Copyright © 2008 Translation from the French by Janis A. Mayes
Copyright © Introduction and Interview – Janis A. Mayes

This edition published by Ayebia Clarke Publishing Limited
7 Syringa Walk
Banbury
OX16 1FR
Oxfordshire
UK

© Éditions L'Harmattan, 1990 (original French version: *Le Royaumme Aveugle*).
First published in English in the UK by Ayebia Clarke Publishing Limited, 2008.
This edition © Ayebia Clarke Publishing Ltd.

Distributed in Africa, Europe & the UK by TURNAROUND at
www.turnaround-uk.com
And distributed outside Africa, Europe and the United Kingdom exclusively by
Lynne Rienner Publishers, Inc.
1800 30th St., Ste. 314
Boulder, CO 80301
USA
www.rienner.com

Co-published in Ghana with the Centre for Intellectual Renewal
56 Ringway Estate, Osu, Accra, Ghana.
www.cir.com

British Library Cataloguing-in-Publication Data.

A catalogue record of this book is available from the British Library.

Cover design by Amanda Carroll at Millipedia.
Cover artwork images © Véronique Tadjo.

Typeset by FiSH Books, Enfield, Middlesex.
Printed and bound in Great Britain by Cox & Wyman Ltd., Reading, Berkshire.

The publisher wishes to acknowledge the support of Arts Council Funding.

ISBN 978-0-9555079-1-5

…o available from www.ayebia.co.uk or email info@ayebia.co.uk

Citation/Epigraph

"...All the anguish of the chest sufferer confined to a narrow room, of the miner who wants to go back to the light, and of the man diving for pearls who feels the whole darkness of the sea weighting on him! All the oppression felt by Plautus or by Samson pushing the millstone, by Sisyphus rolling the rock; all the suffering of a people choking under slavery – these agonies among others, all of them, I have known."

André Gide *Paludes (translated from the French by Janis A. Mayes)*

"If the story I am telling is true, they have told the truth. If it is not true, I have not lied, they have lied."

An Akan saying.

"Here hope has gone, only anger remains."

Words painted on a building in Calcutta.

Part
One

Chapter 1
Earth Jolts

The earth jolted, violently – all of a sudden – while most inhabitants still slept. In a matter of seconds, the world turned upside down. The ground split open, trees fell, walls shifted and collapsed, stones rolled around, torrents of dust darkened the new morning.

The ground trembled, furiously. The earth revolted. Everything appeared to sink into an immense abyss. Sleepers awakened into the middle of a nightmare. Roofs crumbled down on their shoulders; wailing destroyed their throats; panic seized their entire being … Then the world's belly burst open. An atrocious heat bore down. Death knocked and the sky remained merciless.

From everywhere, those who survived got out from the ruins screaming out of fright and running in every direction. Mothers fled with their newborn babies; old people staggered; children crawled around; men shouted out commands.

Dogs barked incessantly. Livestock escaped from their pens. Horses went crazy. No one knew where to go. Fear, and it was a disfiguring fear, sculpted faces.

In a lightning flash, the empire had collapsed. They found themselves hurled into the same fear, the same fate.

Moaning stabbed the atmosphere. People died by the thousands, crushed under ruins, lost in crevices, drowned in the river's muddy waters that flowed, flooded and swept across the land with thunderous sounds. Beings and things floundered in the water, fell and disappeared beneath the surge.

Within seconds, glory was destroyed; the past disemboweled; riches annihilated.

But what followed was worse. When the earth stopped

jolting, finally, and the inhabitants were left facing each other, fear became unbearable. The terror of destruction took hold and paralyzed them, totally.

Horror asphyxiated them. Awareness of the end of the world froze their consciousness. They ranted and raved. They muttered unintelligible words.

And then – all of a sudden – the slaves began the work of digging out. They were the only ones who still had strength to react. With their bare hands, they dug through the debris and handed over the bodies: entombed children; vanished mothers; injured fathers. They called out the names. They waited. They dug. Like prehistoric people, they were at nature's mercy.

Gradually, the others awakened from their heavy inertia. The memory of what had once made up their lives, pushed them to move. They gazed at each other, went down on all fours, and dug. When they were able to get someone out, they felt like they had conquered death.

Clouds of loneliness and despair colored the days – the tears – the distress. How many more days? Time stood still. They looked only to survive – to eat and sleep – tightly holding on to each other, hoping that the new day would come for them, once again.

No longer were there any chiefs, no aristocracy either. No longer were there slaves. People had lost their vanity, their hierarchies, their injustice.

Death had taught them a lesson in humility. Death had shown them her unrivaled might by swallowing whomever she wanted.

No more stratification. No more empire. Simply men and women such as they were at the beginning of time.

This is when, coming from the other side of the mountains, the BlindPeople arrived.

The survivors saw them approaching in a solid mass. Their army was sparkling. Dazzling rays of light streamed from their missiles and firearms. Their power was unmatched; their superiority invincible.

Within a short while, they invaded the empire and installed their kingdom.

unity
vulnerability

4

Chapter 2

The King's Palace

Built on a gigantic hill, the palace spread its wings over the city like a monstrous bat.

The huge room with a hundred mirrors where the king held court formed the body of the beast and its wings were the raised ballrooms where banquets and meetings were held; the king's chambers and those of his daughter were located in the head of the creature. They jutted out and were decorated with fine fabrics and gold encrusted ceilings. At the top of this structure, surveillance radars scanned the kingdom and picked up every sound-wave that moved across the realm.

A bat was carved on the throne and the royal scepter because the bat inhabits the night and masters the sky despite blind eyes. Because the bat with its mysterious cries is the possessor of infinite powers. Because darkness is the bat's force.

Bats lived freely in the gardens of the palace. City-dwellers heard them from afar especially at the king's consecrated feeding time. He stood up straight among them and followed the rustling of their beating wings. He knew, exactly, the special way they sounded if they liked the mixture of ripe fruit, fresh vegetables and insects he threw to them.

These creatures multiplied at an uncontrollable rate. In this way, they colonized all the trees in the city and drove away the sparrows which fled, gradually, towards the North. They attacked the children, getting entangled in their hair. They scratched and emitted piercing cries like needles on eardrums.

Every morning servants washed down the palace's steps and facade. They had to rub, scrape and scrub to get rid of the excrement that these flying mammals left everywhere.

The atmosphere was invaded by a stifling stench and the gardens resembled garbage dumps. Green and blue flies buzzed up around the ears of His Majesty Ato IV.

While feeding his bats one particular day the king was pensive. In the evening he was to host a huge marriage banquet with the entire court in attendance. Normally, this should have put him in a good mood yet he was very unhappy because he would have preferred to spend all this money in honor of his own daughter. His only child. But she categorically refused to get married so instead he had to celebrate the wedding festivities of a young cousin. He was thinking:

"Ahh, how I would have loved to marry off Akissi!" Ato IV was thinking as he returned to his chambers. I would have had made for her a silk dress pearled with the world's largest diamonds and I would have placed on her head a crown of rubies and emeralds.

I do not understand my child, my own daughter. She hides her lovers. I should have been able to persuade her to accept a man of my choosing, but to what good? This would have been pain wasted. If she is the king's daughter, it is by way of her seething blood. If I impose someone on her, she will cloister herself inside her chambers never to leave again."

Ato IV mounted the central staircase, slowly, reproaching himself for not having brought up his daughter as it should have been done. The governesses had not known how to be firm. Not one of them had managed to take charge of her.

"She is just like her mother – (Pssth, he sucked his teeth) this woman from the Great North, this woman with unparalleled intelligence. She had to go. Never ever would I share power! It is passed along bloodlines, and Akissi is my only heir. Flesh of my flesh. Blood of my blood."

The king sighed, trying to calm himself:

"In any case, this is of no importance, or rather: I should have had a son as tradition demands. With a son, I would have conquered the entire world! But why did life decide otherwise? The women who stretched out in my bed – all of them – had wombs as empty as a gourd with holes! Dry, ungrateful wombs, carriers of still-born babies. The people had started to gossip."

Entering his chambers, he exclaimed:

"The slum-dwellers must be kept in awe by the splendor and luxuriousness of the festivities. The cortege will move across the city with all the fanfare. Gold and silver will dazzle their eyes. I want people to be talking still, in one hundred years, about this wedding party! And what's more, in the most remote regions. One must proclaim to the world and to the slum-dwellers that the kingdom has never before been this prosperous! I am going to show them, I, Ato IV, what power is! And one day, it will be my daughter's turn. Then, I will make the entire world tremble with envy! The ceremony feast will be so grandiose that the power of my name will surpass the borders of the Universe! And everyone will know that my reign is limitless and that my throne is cast in solid gold !

Because I am the one who created this country. I, who built it with my own hands, shaped it according to my own will. I am the one who made from its mire and chaos this grandiose site! I am the one who gave it prosperity, strength and eternal life.

Without me, there would be nothing here.

Without me, everyone would have starved.

I am the rock on which the kingdom is built.

I am the king of steel whose power generates the future.

I am the one whose voice makes the mountains tremble.

The one who stops time.

The one who governs.

By day as well as by

Night!"

Chapter 3

The Blind Wedding Party

The orchestra struck up the king's hymn. In one fell swoop, all of the courtesans stood up and the heavy doors of the Festivity Room swung open. "His Majesty Ato IV!"

Bursts of applause struck the walls and rose above the percussion instruments' deafening sounds. Someone shouted: "Long live the king!" And hundreds of voices responded at the top of their voices, "Long live the king!"

Taking small steps and helped by his assistant, the Minister of Armies, the king was led to the head table. The cheering doubled in intensity and the entire room vibrated to the sound of "Ato, Ato, Ato!"

The king then commanded the audience to be silent. When everyone stood still and only the flies continued to flit, he announced, loudly and clearly:

"May the festivities begin!"

At that very moment, the servants made their entrance, laden with dishes emitting irresistible aromas. Fine wines, imported from the most famous cellars in the world, were served in crystal glasses.

Dishes were served uninterrupted for several hours. The waiters' faces were tense as they changed the plates, replaced tableware and brought out new dishes. Wine flowed freely. Conversations were animated. The party was in full swing.

Standing behind each BlindPerson, a server watched carefully over every detail.

Within a split second, the dinner could take a catastrophic turn if, inadvertently, a glass was overturned or if a piece of tableware fell on the marble floor. All conversation would stop and yield to a loud silence. The guests, as if terrorized, would be frozen by the sudden reminder of their blindness.

In the kitchens, the cooks were overwhelmed. Sweat trickled down their foreheads and their oily hands worked rapidly. A piece of overcooked meat, a dish too salty or too bland could cost them their job.

Through the windows that opened onto the courtyard, the sweepers and all of the other palace workers watched with interest the frenetic activities in the kitchens. They waited for the dirty plates and leftovers. As soon as they had the chance, they licked up the sauces, cracked meat bones, ate the marrow and delicately sucked fish bones. Tongue lapping sounds alternated with a repertoire of burps, punctuated by "Uuuuhmm! Uuuuhumm! ..."

The plates that came from the banquet were first cleaned by expert plate-lickers then, several minutes later, plunged into hot water, dried and prepared to return to the tables with immaculate white tablecloths.

Laughter and raised voices moved across the huge room. The dinner was a success. Tomorrow the entire country would talk about tonight's feast. By word of mouth, the wildest rumors would circulate.

The young newlyweds embraced. The bride wore a satin dress embroidered with gold threads that to the touch was as soft as a caress. She felt very beautiful. The ten women who helped her get dressed and took turns perfecting her wedding ensemble had told her so. And, although she had never been able to see herself in a mirror, she kept her head held high and her bearing proud.

There was something truly strange about this habit that all the BlindPeople had of dressing as if they could see each other. It was said that their fingers easily replaced their eyes. Just by lightly touching a fabric, they could know its worth. Just by touching a precious stone, they could determine its purity. They even had the capacity to differentiate between colors and they likewise knew measurements. This is how they moved about, almost gracefully, in a world they had constructed for themselves.

The opening notes of a waltz swirled in the air. The banquet was over and the ball was about to begin. The couple took to the floor and started the first dance.

It was perfect timing for the king to leave. He never danced. A king never dances. Neither did Akissi. As soon as she could slip out of these kinds of festivities, she did it quickly. The entire evening, she struggled against boredom. Too much food made her sick. Too much wine made her sad. And what's more, they had her seated next to young men from good families, young long toothed wolves; or, next to her father's loyal followers. She was not fooled by this strategy and that put her in a bad mood. She would have knocked them senseless with a bottle of champagne every one of these young turkeys, all from the same yard, who talked non-stop and whose breath smelled heavily of alcohol. She was bored to the point of tears, to the point of knocking her head against the walls.

Alone in her room, tucked in her big bed, Akissi awaited sleep that didn't come. She dreamed about the newlyweds, or more precisely, about the groom. She knew him very well. There was a time when they exchanged soft words and when she believed in him. She found him different from the others. She liked what he said because she seemed to learn a lot in his company. He talked to her about the poverty of the slum-dwellers and about the famine that sometimes ravaged the Great North. She had thirstily drunk his words. She had told herself that the truth would finally unveil itself to her. Come to think of it, wasn't he the one who had planted the first seeds of her boredom in this palace?

And now today, ironically, she had attended his marriage! But, anyway, what did it matter? A lot of water had flowed under the bridge since that time and he was no longer the same man. She had taken a while to realize this. He hadn't stood the test. His words had turned out to be empty and without a future. He said one thing and did another. Money had gradually turned his head. After having hesitated, he finally took a path towards power.

"Yet, things aren't as simple as that," Akissi told herself. "What does one do with one's life when one has but one? One must be strong in order to set about doing whatever it is and leave behind the lethargy that paralyzes the body and soul. It is so easy to stay where you were born."

"Here I am, making excuses for him, now," she exclaimed indignantly. "Once again, I'm thinking about our past conversations ... Where is the truth? Where is the truth when it is so easy to know nothing? "Akissi buried her face in the pillow and sighed.

When she slept, she dreamed about her father and she had nightmares. It was always the same one that came back. The ground was strewn with corpses. The king's mutilated body was lying in the dust. His severed head was impaled on a spear in the middle of the garden. There was blood. Blood everywhere. Blood that ran down the main staircase. Smoking hot blood. A bat alighted on his head and devoured his eyes.

Akissi woke up sweating. She knew all too well what this nightmare meant: the end was near. Why then didn't he want to understand? Didn't he know that now he had to relinquish his position? Corruption, greed, wastefulness, everything ate away at the kingdom.

The reign fell apart and yet, the courtesans continued to sing praise-songs. The praises increased, glorifying the present and abolishing the future.

Akissi could take it no longer. Where to go to escape this turmoil, to protect herself? Was being the king's daughter the sin she had committed in her mother's womb?

Where to go to escape the lies and madness of an entire horde of BlindPeople?

Chapter 4

To find Mother, again

Mother. She had to find her lost mother. Who was she? Where to draw in her memory, the taste of her mother's milk, the smell of her breast? Head buried in her bosom. Eyes closed. Where is Mother?

To find Mother. To find the first love you are searching for you must go further and further until you find happiness by melting into someone else, recognizing yourself in someone else's skin, consoling yourself with someone's warmth. To find Mother, again. To look for her everywhere where she can be found. To stop the cold winter of isolation. To stop the distress of being alone.

Chapter 5

The Inhuman City

The city stretched out its entire full length. It was everywhere. The view was unending with the sight of buildings and structures that blocked the horizon. From left to right, concrete enclosed, oppressed, imprisoned.

An immense mural of hills surrounded the city and one could also believe that they marked its borders. But no, life still extended well beyond. Wooden shanties in clusters clung to each other and, each day, edged a little more ground. These were the slums where the OtherPeople lived.

Vehicles came and went, like worker ants. And nothing could break this stream of engines sending grey lightning flashes of steel that bounced against the sky's ceiling and disfigured the city.

A dirty layer of dust hung over the roofs and stopped the sun from piercing through. It seemed that night was always ready to fall. All the walls appeared to be faded.

The BlindPeople were detached from all of that. The sky, the sun, the trees were not made for them. They were abstractions, simple abstractions that evoked no image in their dead imagination.

The OtherPeople, the only ones to go around town on foot, coughed, spat, choked. And what's more, being in the city was like being in a sand-storm, a thick fog clouded the view.

And yet, the city grew more and more each day. The slum-dwellers moved to the hills like an army in rags preparing to seize the enemy. Small rickety shanties were all attached, planted like turfs of dry grass. They resembled dark warts jolting up from the ground: abnormal bumps drowned in a mixture of smoke and poison.

Some mornings, the police descended into these poor areas. Bludgeoning and yelling, armed men broke down doors with their dreadful boots. In less than fifteen minutes, everything was turned upside down, and trucks loaded with men, still sleepy eyed, drove away with horns blaring, towards the prisons.

Smoke rose slowly from the factories in operation. Contaminated air burned nostrils and infected lungs. When there was wind, the clouds moved and the air cooled slightly. But that wind was terrible. It dried up everything. Skin cracked and faces aged. The grass became so yellow that it resembled a harvest moon landscape. Trees were skinny and tired. The ground stayed whitish.

Yet, in this lost city, some birds that refused to abandon it still remained. In the midst of chaos, they chirped and sang, vying in turn with one another. When evening fell, twittering was heard from high perched nests. It was as if people had admitted their defeat and given up their hopes to the sparrows.

It had not always been like that. There was a time when the city possessed another history, a great past that the BlindPeople had destroyed.

This was the time of profound traditions and mystical societies. Art held a high position then and dance celebrated every festivity. Men wore costumes in divine colors: a mixture of the sacred and the mundane. They made beautiful statues and dwellings constructed with mud and compact clay.

It was the time of gods and of magic. The time of ancestral beliefs. The time also of lines and colors that wedded with the sky in rays of pure clarity. .

But, all was destroyed: bas-reliefs, giant statues, clay pots and earthenware. Everything was destroyed. All of these patiently made treasures were broken, plundered, thrown away.

Ahhh, if only the empire had not known injustice; slavery! If only the empire had been united!

From that point on, history was made up of fierce oppression. Slums multiplied like cockroach nests. And the OtherPeople struggled, pitifully. There was no patch of grass, no place to rest and feel that life was worth the pain of living. Between the wooden shanties, trickles of slimy water carried the stench of blistering hot days. Hungry dogs spent their days on rubbish-strewn wasteland.

Everything was grey. Everything was sad. Worn out clothing trembled on clothes-lines.

No electricity. When darkness came, fires were lit here and there. Flaming bits of wood made a flickering light. Skin and hair smelled of smoke. Strange food cooked in clay pots.

In vain, the slum-dwellers had tried to recreate village life. Animals roamed freely among them and entered wherever they wanted. No one had secrets. Life was out in the open.

Yet, there was no peace and there was no hope either. No rain, no good weather either. People felt withered by life.

In these slums, childhood did not stand a chance. Impossible for the little ones to have children's dreams and childish games. They were little men and women with battered hearts.

Misery crawled at the speed of a cursed snake and infected entire areas. The OtherPeople gathered on the hills and awaited the impossible. Each morning they left for the city that swallowed up their life.

But at times, some of them would decide to run away from the slums, to leave everything behind them to go to live among the BlindPeople. In so doing, they blacked out their past and swore never to remember any of it. They closed their eyes so as not to recall anything. It was they who haunted the palace corridors and who swelled the army's ranks. Without them, the BlindPeople would never have been able to live out their reign.

Who were they?

What did they want?

What did they hope for, these people who played with fire?

Chapter 6

The Man with a strong scent

He had looked at her for quite a long while with his very round, carbon-black eyes. This was a handsome, lithe man. His body had a sensual scent and he laughed often to the point of breathlessness.

He laughed; he laughed; he laughed so much that she wondered whether he wasn't a little sad. She pretended as though she had not noticed him, but in reality, she was perfectly conscious of his presence. This had happened without any effort; one day, he was right there and she could no longer pretend not to know it.

He had looked at her for quite a long while with his very round, carbon-black eyes. And she felt his steady gaze.

It was her governess who brought it to her attention that she had an admirer. She asked right away: "Who is it?" And the governess replied: "It's Karim, the king's new secretary." Then, she said, "Describe him to me." And the woman talked about his very round pupils and svelte body. As for the scent, Akissi already knew. But when she learned that he came from the vast land of the OtherPeople, she could not hide her confusion … "From the Great North!?, she asked totally perplexed, before sinking into a long silence.

That particular morning, Akissi walked up and down the huge rooms of the palace. Hands behind her back, she was in deep thought. She frowned, lips tight.

The king had summoned her, but she had not gone to his side. She knew what he was going to ask her to do: to tell a story.

Every morning, it was the same thing. Today, she didn't feel like doing it one bit. He said that she had a magnificent voice that he would never get tired of. He said that she was such a good storyteller that it kept him in a good mood for the rest of the day. He said that this made him forget the solitude that comes with power.

"He feels old," she thought. "Yes, that's it, he feels old. They can talk as much as they want throughout the kingdom about his most recent mistress, a heavily perfumed courtesan ... umh, me, Akissi, I am not stupid. That woman is for show! She wears jewels and spends huge amounts of money, but as for the rest ..."

The king, the king, always the king! Akissi wanted rather to save her thoughts for someone else. Karim, being her father's secretary, what kind of man could he be?

The secretary before him had embezzled so much money that one day, he just took off. The stuffed envelopes that he distributed to the courtesans on the king's behalf were not as full as they should have been. How would Karim be?

Akissi was not pleased. Why did life seem to be so complicated? She finally met someone whom she truly liked and it had to be her father's secretary!

Days went by and Akissi dreamed of Karim. That's all that she did. He mesmerized her. She went to bed and woke up with the memory of him. She attended to her activities while thinking of him. She told herself that she would love to be near him, to touch him and sail in this infinite tenderness that filled her heart. She had only one desire: to caress his skin and to discover at long last the contours of his body.

But he could see her just as she was! That frightened her. And to think she had never been concerned with her appearance! Her governess told her over and over again that she was beautiful, but was this the truth?

"Have I gone completely mad?" She asked herself in order to regain her self control. "I hardly know him and I am already so wrapped up!"

17

She longed to talk to him. Tell him what was in her heart: how much she felt a prisoner of her own blindness and of the thoughts that bumped up against the vault of her conscience. She felt like a prisoner of her entire being, locked up in itself, confined in her flesh and, when all was said and done, alone. She inhabited a darkness where others were merely ghosts of stone.

She did not know where she put her feet; did not know where she went. No path to guide her way, no horizon for her to reach. She wandered into a desert of infinite sand dunes and her feet dug into the sand that slowed down her daily rhythm.

Her blindness was her greatest failure; her inability to see life such as it was in the raw sunlight; to see things face to face. She was aware of all of this and made herself miserable by knowing. Was she going to keep holding out her hands in front of her for fear of falling? Was this the price of a life without courage, a life dragging behind days and years?

Most often, she left it to others to organize her life, and left it to chance to avoid making decisions reacting only when she found her back against the wall. Events led her here and there; balancing her destiny like a tree branch swinging in the wind. Was she capable of being deeply committed to anything? She always had within herself this uncontrollable desire to hold back her enthusiasm; to break up her urge so as to avoid going too far.

But now she was tired of all of these debilitating precautions. She was tired of living in slow motion and sparing her emotions.

Soon, she would not have much time left. What good does it serve to take no risks, incessantly weighing the pros and cons? What would she make of her life? What would she have accomplished in 10 years? In 20 years?

She knew that she was knowledgeable about many things: dates, facts, history and stories; the mechanics of life and laws of nature. She only knew palace life; but to her credit, she had more than skin-deep sensitivity and a desire to hear the truth.

And it was this desire to hear the truth that tortured her and made her weary, because she knew that in this palace where lying and betrayal were customary, there was nothing there to quench her thirst or open her eyes. Nothing to cure her of anemia.

Akissi wanted to tell Karim how much she already needed him; about how unique and important he was to her. She wanted to get closer to this passion that she felt throbbing in him and that proved he was alive.

She knew the decadence of the kingdom and she knew that with the courage to confront life, she would be capable of discovering the colors of existence and of reality. She could well imagine what he would say if he found himself in front of her. He would say, "Why do you ask yourself so many questions, yet, you never act, never lift up your head?" And then he would say again, "What is stopping you from leaving, from breaking down the walls of your prison? Is it fear of discovering your own bare face? "

There was a storm raging in Akissi's head. Her imagination was in a whirlwind and she invented words, phrases, images that danced around Karim. This gave her an unknown strength, a courage that she did not believe she had ever possessed.

So, she pulled together her scattered will and started to live as if something were soon going to explode.

And then, finally, one evening, she asked herself. "It's true, why stay here? Why die from indigestion, why live and die like a balloon bursting in the wind?"

Chapter 7

Words Never Said

"Listen, Father, the wind is blowing backwards, the rains are slow in falling, the grass is dry. The sun is at war.

Listen closely to what I am going to say to you. I will not speak again. Maybe you will hear me in the silence.

Listen, for a long time, I have been waiting to say these words which have never come out of my mouth...

I am worried about you. Because of your trembling voice, because of your hands that are no longer firm. But, there is a wall between us. We are unknown to each other. All my life, I have lived by your side; and yet, we do not know each other. We have been cloistered together in one world without ever becoming close.

This wall between us is larger than ever now, I no longer recognize the sound of your voice. I know that you are aging and that because of it you are suffering. I know that you are feeling alone, even in my presence. We have known nothing of each other for such a long time.

The wall frightens me now because time is pressing and days are passing in a flash. We cannot go back and change anything. Those words would have been enriching, exchanges that would have brought us closer together, gestures that would have made us live again.

But why am I such a coward. Why didn't I know how to make it better?

For such a long time this running away, this interminable race right next to you made me weary.

Now that I am a woman I am worried for you and tell myself that my strength should serve some purpose. Do you still remember the one day we played together when you came to me and you became so immersed in my child play and games? Do you remember how your chest puffed out from very loud laughter?

Father, your absences hurt me. Your words disturb me. The words that we exchange have neither substance nor fragrance. You hide and I do not know where to find you. Will you tell me one day that you love me?

Listen, it is simple. These are bad times. I no longer have faith. If we don't want to construct war, we must build peace. At least I know that. Nothing else counts. You must change.

I thirst for a life where to sleep with closed fists is not a sign of weakness. A life written in bold letters, clean and with nothing crossed out.

Father! Father! For too long you have reigned with fury. You have fashioned a kingdom in the way that pleased you. You have spoken on behalf of everyone and the voices were made quiet so that each one of us could hear you.

Now, it is you who is to be silent and sit in a corner of history.

Listen, this is important: I am leaving!"

Chapter 8

Karim's Secret

Some nights, Karim and his companions went in secret to visit the slum-dwellers. After having washed thoroughly and changed clothes, they left behind the BlindPeoples' palace to plunge into a world that they knew well. The one where they spoke the same language as the others and where they could laugh, discuss and plan until dawn.

This was in the form of long meetings during which they were seated in a circle each person rising in turn to say what was in his heart and on his mind. Karim listened. Karim spoke. Karim learned what was essential and took in many fertile thoughts.

Everything happened in the sound and festive gathering of voices. An extraordinary sound that never went beyond the borders of the slum. Laughter and clapping of hands.

Karim felt tied to them at the navel. With them, he found once again a reason for living, deep motivations from all of his bitter years and personal sacrifices. He was there to trace new directions with them and to be enlightened by their words on his perilous journey.

Karim thus lived a double life that helped him to advance and continue. Living was still burdensome and overwhelming but at least he was not dead. His soul remained intact, his reasoning always alert. He had stayed the same; the child of the savanna, the little one with the balloon-stomach who ran around on the arid land. He had remained the son of the dust and of the red soil, the protégée of spirits of dry wind.

He knew well that life for him in the palace was harmful. He wanted to stop everything, and have this monstrous edifice exploded. But he refused to lose his head and struggled with all the force that he had against this violence that seemed to rise up in him.

Blood, blood! Never to know the smell of blood! Never to be the one through whom horror would enter into the country, but to be the one to inscribe in white the name of new found freedom! Freedom like a river that flows, that ripples, its silver scales sparkling, smooth, fluid, musical and calm. Freedom without murders, without executions, without courts, nor torture. Freedom: in successive bursts of energy, by collective will.

But sometimes these meetings took another turn that planted anguish in Karim's spirit. "Enough!" screamed some of the slum-dwellers. "We must topple the walls of the palace! We must shatter the throne!" And when they spoke like this their faces expressed profound revulsion and their bodies were tight and knotted up. "We must bring this to an end! Destroy this cursed kingdom! Burn this wretched city!" they shouted again. It was obvious that they had suffered and that each word pronounced shredded their throats. But it was the outrage that aroused them and no one could do anything about it.

How does one explain, Karim wondered, how does one make it understood that the goal is not to kill, but to create? To build, to make up for lost time, to make a life for everyone. Karim believed in a kingdom where neither palace nor slum would be built. But how does one find the words to arrest the hopelessness of those who were tired of waiting? He only had promises to give them and an uncertain future to propose. He tried to calm them down with words of hope but they answered him back: "Hurry up, because our patience is running out. It's today and not tomorrow that we want to live!"

At the time there lived a prophet, a poet, a storyteller, an orator, an enigma, who moved tirelessly throughout the slums. Everywhere he went, people said that he was mad; they said that he was wise; they said that his loose tongue knew countless poems, songs, proverbs and many other things, too, and that he had a particular way of saying them; of singing them with such conviction. His voice was a deep bass which was pleasing to hear. And it inspired a longing for more.

Everything about him was geared towards storytelling: his face bore many expressions; his gestures and his head of hair prompted some people to say that he was mad because it formed an entangled compact mass that he never combed.

He carried within himself an incredible fervor that was the engine driving his actions. It was intrinsic to him, rooted in the very depth of his being and always rose to the surface when he spoke about serious matters. In such rare moments, his voice took on a quality of steel and a tone of combativeness. His gaze hardened. An unfathomable grimace overtook his face.

Everywhere he went, the prophet fascinated people with the sheer number of his tales and images. He carried a big sack over his shoulder, and when he put it down on the ground and plunged his hand into it, he always brought out a poem, a song or beautiful words to hear. Whether it was day or night, he could do it. People woke him up when there was a full moon, and he would get up, plunge his hand into his sack and bring out a story. And the same thing at high noon when the sun was very hot, he always brought something out that was pleasing to hear.

So he walked throughout the city's slums living on very little, because he never asked for anything. He only wanted to be heard. Then, he would say to those who truly wanted to hear him, many words of truth. One day he declared: "I know that everything passes and that our life is only held together by a thread. Lightning could strike in one second and everything is over. Anger can destroy everything. The solitude that is crushing us is not the only truth of our reality. We can transform hell into purgatory. When I touch someone and it does me good, I know that I am getting there. When I close my eyes and I still see love, I know that I am getting there.

Everything is uncertain; everything is transitory; everything is not enough. Yesterday, we proudly stuck out our chests and today, our hands are trembling, and we are no longer sure of

24

anything. Yesterday, everything seemed to be in order; today time is battling against us.

We must learn how to subdue the suffering; learn how to tame the pain; accept that our outrage is to be retained. It must be beautiful and complete; powerful and fertile. We need outrage in order to keep living and the courage to conquer evil-doing."

The prophet looked all around the crowd that encircled him. Some of them had their eyes opened wide; and others looked worried. But, as it was very hot, the slum-dwellers started to leave one after the other. The storyteller felt a sharp chest pain. He felt tired and his throat dried up. "Come back!" he shouted. "I have not finished." And some people came back. Someone wiped his forehead and brought him a glass of water. After he had had enough to drink, he picked up the thread of his speech.

"There are some people who are subdued and already beaten by death. They have a pitiful look in their eyes and sad faces. Some people decide to willingly carry the burden of the world on their shoulders; some people let the devil dance until he can dance no more. Then there are some people like that, who always think of taking second place and who are content with crumbs.

The slum-dwellers moved closer to the poet and listened intently. The speaker was courageous. He did not mince his words, did not back down before a crowd. Even if the people were busy living a useless life, he always found a way to make them think. Because he himself was searching for something and this something, he had not yet found.

It was during one of his secret visits to the city slums that Karim, who had been walking in an open field, found himself face to face with the mad prophet. In the semi-darkness of evening, the two men looked each other up and down for a long time. The moon beamed an eerie light. All of a sudden the storyteller took several quick steps backward and pointed an accusing finger in the visitor's direction.

"You wear your passion like a crown made of thorns. You want to save the world and you think that your crucifixion will change the course of history. Beware! If you fight alone, you will die alone – or, with a few lonely comrades – what difference would it make? Do not return to that palace where your life is being torn to shreds. Do not return to that ruined palace where darkness clouds the horizon. There you will find hell."

Karim stood still as if petrified by the storyteller's words. He broke into a cold sweat. His heart started to beat intensely. He closed his eyes to regain his composure, to calm his panic-stricken body. When he opened them again, the speaker had disappeared.

So, he continued his walk to the congregated wooden shanties. His feet stumbled over stones and various objects that were strewn all over the ground. A pile of trash emitted a nauseating fecal smell. The air was filled with dust.

Part
Two

Chapter 9

Karim and Akissi

His body was as smooth as a lagoon in the sun. She was shaped like sand dunes along the seashore.

His skin stretched out to eternity with grains of sand everywhere, forming a delicate and smooth mosaic on which her hands moved round and round, went up and down; caressed and tenderly touched.

Her body was made of curves and fragile flesh; her breasts moving softly; her belly ready to welcome life.

They were there, side by side: he, locked in his passion draped in his unbelievable arrogance; she, with all her senses unhinged and a very proud heart. One could see on his face that this was a man who knew what suffering was; who sometimes descended to the depths of the earth, to the place where the only thing to be heard was the soil breathing. His face had signs of aging. And he even had a few strands of unconcealed white hair.

On her face, you could see no tell-tale signs. Not yet.

It was only her blind eyes that you noticed at first. But, elsewhere, there were other revealing signs: maybe her waist which was a little thick; maybe a few spider veins appearing here and there.

She, with volatile strength and open hands, did not yet know the dangers of truth or of the path she was taking.

His body was like a song of the savanna that the wind carries while sweeping the crests of the fields. Dust swirling. He was like a refrain, one of these voices that pierces the light of noon and freshens the scorching heat of the day.

She was a song that begins, but does not end, haunting music that seeps through sleep, dreams and hope.

They were all of that and yet so little at all: two beings side by side.

Chapter 10

Love

The man speaks:

"Open your thighs. Let's ride and ride... Your body is a storm, a tidal wave I drown in to die and be born again as much as you want. I am digging deep inside you a fertile tunnel where my seed will germinate. And I live and relive in your damp darkness my wildest dreams: where I only want you and you only want me; where my only strong urge is to break through the secrets of your body. Your body which swallows me, sweeps me up and carries me far, far away.

Give me your body and let mine go into yours so that they turn and twirl and embrace each other to the point of exhaustion.

Offer me once more the gift of your narrow opening.

The woman speaks:

Come, I want to make love under the open sky. My skin quivers when you touch it. My nerves are on edge. My breath is taken away.

Come, sail as far as you want on the waves of my passion which has no name and flows inside me like a mighty river.

Come, to forget that maybe tomorrow we will be parted.

Come, to forget that your power has penetrated my soul,

Come, I am giving myself to you just as I am and I am calling you,

I am calling you."

Chapter 11

Making love with her eyes closed

She made love with her eyes closed, prisoner of her infirmity, prisoner of her body which showed her nothing of the sky or the earth. So, she gave herself wholly, pulled by a force that was a hundred times stronger that she; a force that took her deep down into a strange enclosed space where everything was comprised only of smells, whispers and sounds; where the skin was alive and warm, crossed over by hot, trembling caresses; where liquids mixed with fluids; saliva with sweat; and where the mouth was filled with taste, filled with wanting and desire.

She let herself be taken away by the body she discovered in every slow, deep turn. More and more, she lost her footing and was just a creature clinging to love and letting herself live from within. So with each movement, something like a deep swelling, a furious sea, she let herself be carried away. She was floating adrift like a lost raft.

And Karim's hands touched her skin; molded it. And in the dark blackness of her body, she took on every shape and form: woman-mermaid; woman-goddess; demon-angel or giver of life, and in her soul she cried out: "Karim are you a mountain or a lion; triumphant or destructive?"

In the depth of her love, she was afraid. Her inner strength escaped and slid into him. What would become of her? Vulnerable to everything around her, and also to him who could crush her if he wanted to?

As she gave herself to him, it was her soul she offered; her heart; her life. She wished she could melt then merge with his flesh to become one, to be sure that he would not leave her; to be sure that they would never be strangers to one another.

She gripped him, holding on squeezing him tightly, very tightly. And their skins blended and the smell of their bodies flooded them with pleasure and love.

And this was a cry from within that she let out when everything inside her dissolved and she was carried away to sea.

Chapter 12

The Lovers' Night

Karim and Akissi spent the whole night talking to each other and holding hands. They talked about everything, of the past and the future. They laughed often like children and they asked each other many questions. Then when they felt sleepy, they would doze with their bodies pressed close together breathing in rhythmic harmony. After a while, they would wake up, start talking and asking each other more questions that they played at answering or not answering. They would say things that were unimportant and the next second talk in a serious tone which made them realize they were unveiling dangerous secrets. But the night was for them unending and the pleasure they found in discovering they were together was priceless.

They talked at length, even though at times, they were scared by what they confided in each other. They had decided not to mince their words, their claims, their ideas and their answers. They chose to try to be understanding and to dismantle, with patience, the mechanics of loneliness.

Later she revealed to him her fears, and her will to change. She told him about her desire to leave.

He tried to calm her anxiety by whispering words of comfort, but he saw that she was still worried and that her face had clouded over. He then felt filled with compassion for this girl who attempted to leave the closed world of her birth and who while feeling her way took her first steps in the open. He told himself that maybe he should not have let her in when she had come knocking at his door. With him, her life was going to take a different turn altogether. Did she really know what she had committed to? Was she ready to renounce all of her privileges and the slow pace of time? She thought she was able to struggle, but would she have the strength to go all the way to the end of her quest?

Karim took Akissi's face into his hands and kissed her lips. The young woman's eyes remained fixed looking into empty space, transparent like flowing water. "Yes," he pondered,

"It's worth it to try. Anything, except this stare that doesn't say anything!"

He told her in a raised voice:

"It's not by fleeing your country that you will understand things better. It is here that you will find the answers to the questions you are asking yourself. Go to the Great North. I know where you can hide there."

Hearing these words, Akissi's smile reappeared and everything inside her became calm and serene again.

When he felt her heart unburdened, in a strong and invigorating voice, he revealed to her a vision which had come to him one day.

"I had a daydream where I saw the kingdom all stretched out in front of me. This was no longer a kingdom, but a free territory where people were walking in peace. There were no more BlindPeople; nor we, the OtherPeople. There was no longer any opulence nor any misery, but a fair sharing. You see, what truly matters is when we are together and we make one. One day or the other, we are going to rebuild this country and open the way for a possible future."

"You see," he added, "there are no two ways about this: either the kingdom regenerates itself or it dies! "

Chapter 13

Burning/ regenerating

"**B**URNING: the sun will split in two and blazing liquid will pour onto the soil. Everything will burn. The earth will become blood-red and the iron ore will shoot up from below and arrows will fly in all directions, and, suddenly, animals everywhere will be transfixed and it will be as if nothing had ever existed."

But the people will not die. Their flesh will have burned naked. Fire will parch their throats. They will be facing the void, a never-ending temptation. And they will want to be done with it when their breathing stops. They will drown in their own anguish.

But they will never know the end of fear, this sharp blade that cuts one's spirit. They will start to turn on each other and howl in the burnt air, but nothing will appease their suffering and there will no longer be signs of life anywhere, except in them, horrible puppets, cursors of life, demonic puppets, pillagers, thieves, destroyers who did not know that one day, all of this would end, that their days would be numbered and that the sun would split in two to pour its blazing liquid on them.

REGENERATING: to find the strength to change; to start all over again, in order to cancel out the past leaden with mistakes and multiple errors.

To live again, to find a new form. To wash away all filth, to drink water from a new source. To rediscover light in its most potent vividness and in its truest warmth. Going to the roots of the day. To follow the direction of time and shapes of the future.

To sow, to labor, to harvest. To receive from the land the freshest plants and sweetest fruit.

To know how to cast off your worn out skin, your sick habits. To look, hear, touch. To accept, refuse and at last to construct.

At every age to be reborn or die. At every age and even at every moment. Yet, for how long a time will it have to be said over and over again?

Chapter 14

Karim's Bat

"One day when I was descending the palace's grand staircase, I saw a bat which had crashed on the stairs. It was dead. I approached it and looked at it closely. It was on its back, with the head turned slightly to one side, wings spread out.

I could see the beauty of its velvety grey colored stomach. The membrane of its wings was unbelievably soft and opaque, yet, so resistant to pressure from the air and wind. I could not contain the desire to stroke its coat. Its body was still warm and put me in a dream-like state for several seconds.

Its head resembled a dog's with teeth hanging out, and a long muzzle mouth, and big translucent ears. But it was the color of its silky fur that amazed me the most, and also the claws at the extremity of the wings: a mixture of softness and violence; beauty and horror.

Yes, it was one of the bats that sowed panic and anger in the heart of slum-dwellers. One of those animals that, from above, in a sky obscured by their sheer numbers, resembled threatening clouds, animal bearers of evil.

But, who is at fault?

The king has turned them into monstrous beasts that multiply and invade the city. They pillage the trees and excrete their waste well beyond the palace walls. Their shrieking cries are no longer plaintive, but strident, horrible for those people who are in despair from their life of misery and brutality. The life of the forgotten, of the downtrodden, scratched from history, and whose unique privilege is that of sight. Seeing with their own eyes the decadence of the city. Seeing the madness of these BlindPeople who are making their life miserable and playing a hellish game.

People whose unique privilege is their ability to see chaos and madness; to understand that this can no longer be endured. That something has to be done. Now. One way or another."

Chapter 15

Hope is Dead!

The poet speaks:

"A country without hope is a country that is collapsing.
When entire generations cannot succeed and when life dies a little more each day, of a death without burial, without rest, without yesterday,
When columns of men and women find themselves in front of closed doors,
When the day does not exist,
When the sun fades,
Then, they unearth the war hatchet and invoke the Spirit of Thunder.
When those who cultivate the land turn in circles on the arid soil and when the women give birth without joy,
When the rains no longer fall and when the livestock die,
Then, they all rush to the city's gate and curse injustice.
When life is poorly sketched-out, broken down and harsh,
Then, revolt fires up. And the stakes start burning.
Hope is dead! Hope is dead!"

Part
Three

Chapter 16

The Sky of the Great North

The closer one got to the Great North, the clearer the sky became and the purer the air felt. The light changed into a crystal clear blue, so clear that it seemed to verge on pink. Clouds white, like down, drifted softly. One would have said foam from a silent sea. The sun was strong and solid, sovereign and sometimes devastating.

When evening fell, everything became purple and crickets started their vibrating chant. But this was an apogee that did not last a long time, because soon night would come; a night without fault where the stars were points of suspension.

Akissi saw nothing of the landscape. She did not see the savanna nor the ochre-colored soil nor the birds that crossed the sky soaring in full flight. She took a deep breath and all the perfumed scents pervaded through her: those of trees, of tall grass and of burnt earth.

The car traveled over the hard dirt road covering Akissi's hair with dust. Her hands smelled of earth. The man who drove her talked to her about the drought, empty wells and lack of water. She listened and sank into a world that was at the same time close and far away. She asked herself how she could have lived such a long time without knowing this area. In so doing she had mutilated her country and cut her soul into tiny pieces.

She had so much to learn! To till the land when the soil was so hard that it refused to let itself be tamed was an endless struggle. She had heard of the strange ways people from this part of the country cultivated the land. They said that they gathered the earth into small mounds so that the fields looked like blistered skin and pushed in seeds from which thread-like plants sprang forth.

She had also heard of people with backs bent under the sun. They swung their tools to pierce the soil's crust and when it cracked, they sang their victory.

But, from year to year, the land became pitiful, more and more parched, almost sterile. The trees let out cries that were heart breaking. Without rain, the heat ruined everything. Fire scoured the bush and left patches on the soil that were black and uneven.

Akissi ended up by going to sleep nodding off, lulled by the buzzing sound of the engine. Tiny pearls of sweat danced on her face and decorated her lips. A line of salty drops were like sparkles.

The dirt road was tortuous. At times, the high grass hid the view and if the driver had not been from the region, he would have lost his way. You could die out here, far away from villages, if you did not know how to pierce the soil to unearth edible roots, if you did not know how to recognize leaves that you needed to chew in order to quench thirst, if you did not know how to stretch out far away from snakes and hyenas in brown coats.

But the man was at ease in this landscape. Karim had entrusted Akissi to him and he was taking her to the right door.

At the end of the horizon, huge, grandiose boulders appeared like a mirage. And soon, at their feet, there were clusters of round houses with earthen walls and straw roofs that pointed straight up like dots over "i." They were all colors of the soil and crowded together.

The car came to a halting stop, slowed down by rocks that were strewn over the soil. Akissi woke up. She knew that she had arrived. The man took her by the hand and helped her get out. He carefully guided her along the rocky terrain.

The sun was high in the sky. Men and women were in the fields. The village seemed almost deserted. All alone a few old people watched the strangers pass and extended greetings. Some children came to them running and clapping their hands. Akissi heard their joyful noises. She felt a sense of happiness. Had she ever heard laughter this clear?

The walk across the village ended in a court yard. When the husky voice of an old woman reached her ears, Akissi guessed right away that she was in the presence of Karim's mother. Even before shaking her hand, the contact had already been established. And when their hands finally met, the palm of the Old Woman seemed as rugged as the earth. And it was this sensation that went straight to Akissi's heart. She understood that the Old Woman knew the secrets of the soil and that she must certainly have very white hair.

"Welcome, my daughter, the old woman said, and may the spirits protect you!"

"Thank you, mother. I have come all the way to learn from you."

The Old Woman let the two new visitors into her house. The interior smelled of dried tobacco leaves. The air was fresh. They sat down on small stools and the Old Woman placed a calabash of water in front of them.

The man started the discussion. First, he introduced Akissi, shared some news from the city and gave a report on the activities and health of Karim. The Old Woman listened attentively while punctuating his sentences with guttural sounds.

When he finished, the Old Woman spoke in turn about the events of the village: births and deaths. She spoke mostly about the drought.

Finally, the man came to the point of his mission:

"Mother, Karim asks that you welcome Akissi and take care of her as if she were your daughter. Teach her to see. Know, however, that her father is the king Ato IV."

The Old Woman took a long look at Akissi, then she said in a voice filled with kindness:

"That's good. She is already my daughter. When you return to the city, tell Karim that I am waiting for him, that his special woman and I are waiting for him. Tell him that the entire village is waiting for him. That he must not forget us..."

The Old Woman accompanied the man as far as the neighboring courtyard where he had to eat and spend the night before getting back on the road at day break. Akissi found herself alone in the house. She groped for the little suitcase she had brought with her, and was reassured to find it at her side. Inside, there was a little clothing, a little money and her most precious possession: a radio. This was all that linked her from here on to her past life. All of a sudden, she felt very weary. What would she do in this village? How could she one day belong to this land? The people here had such profound roots, but she had none at all. It was not the fruits of harvests that nourished her body. It was not the land that had served as her umbilical cord.

As soon as she returned, the Old Woman installed Akissi into the courtyard and started to prepare their meager evening meal. Akissi listened closely to the surrounding noises. Voices were raised a little everywhere. The men and women had come back from the fields. But their voices seemed unhappy, because they were tired of having worked hard and of having watched the dry earth refuse to produce the necessary quantity of millet with which they nourished themselves and made fermented beer.

Footsteps crossed the courtyard. The Old Woman exchanged greetings. Several people stopped to gaze and talk with her, but no one stayed. A smell of charcoal wood floated in the air. The Old Woman lived alone. She had wanted it that way and the people of the village respected her choice. But she had not been abandoned. They gave her gifts, even in this difficult season: a chicken, a little cassava, some rice or corn. Women especially brought tomatoes, eggplant and salt. Her son also sent her money, but when she received bills that came from the city, she folded them delicately and went to hand them over to the village chief. She did not want to change anything in her life. She preferred to stay in her house where, before his death, her husband joined her at night fall and where, one morning, Karim was born.

Now, the things of her past were sprawled out behind her. Her old age preserved her from passion and from taboos. She was no longer a woman, because she could not give birth. The knowledge of secrets belonged to her. She could approach the Mask and speak the secret language of the initiated.

After the meal, the Old Woman unfolded her mat and stretched it out close to Akissi's. The perfume of incense that burned in the little pot was intoxicating. For Akissi, sleep did not come right away. But when it finally came, it was as heavy as the night.

Chapter 17

Costume made of Straw

Elder Mother, good morning!

> Wishing you fresh air and water!
> May I enter your house?
> How are the people in your courtyard?
> How is your guest?
> How is your tobacco field?
> How is your body feeling?

Hearing the greetings that came from the courtyard, Akissi realized that the Old Woman had been up for a long time. For a few seconds, she wondered where she was. Her back was pressed against the dusty floor and a smell so different from anything she was used to kept her feeling rather lethargic. She did not know whether she should get up or stay put lying there.

How much time was she going to spend here?

Bits and pieces of conversation reached all the way to her. A man had come to see the Old Woman to relay a message from a group of Elders. The Mask was going to come out in a few days.

The Old Woman thanked the messenger. As soon as he was in the distance, she entered the round house to help Akissi get up.

The young woman washed her face with a little water and slowly regained her whereabouts. Her energy came back. The Old Woman gave her a pagne which she tied underneath her arms.

"Come my daughter, I must explain to you what is going to happen soon."

The Old Woman talked while Akissi ate hot millet cereal that slightly burned the tip of her tongue.

"Everyone, even people who are not from the village, must participate in the ceremony by giving an offering to the Mask."

"But mother, what can I offer?" Akissi was worried.

"Calm down, the Old Woman replied, patting her shoulders, today is market-day. We are going together to pick out a little goat. That is the animal preferred by the gods."

"Alright, mother, I will do what seems right to you."

"So, finish eating, because we are leaving right away."

Akissi had stood almost all the way up, when the Old Woman stopped her movement, grabbing her by her arm.

"Wait a second! Before leaving, I want to ask you a question..."

"I'm listening, mother, "Akissi said, a little perplexed.

The Old Woman paused a bit, then asked directly:

"Are you pure, my daughter?"

"Pure...? What do you mean?"

"I mean, is blood running between your legs?"

"No .Why?"

"Because if so, you could not participate in the ceremony."

Akissi was so confused by what she had just heard, that she did not know what to say. The Old Woman kept on talking.

"This is the way it is. A woman can not take part in the ceremonies during that particular period. If she ignores this taboo, she goes completely mad, falls into a trance, and no one can stop it."

"I can assure you that at this moment I am pure," Akissi replied, trying to hide her uneasiness.

The Old Woman seemed satisfied. She quickly arranged the plates and kitchen utensils then they both took the pathway to the market.

The Old Woman took small steps and held Akissi's hand, tightly, as if she feared that she would fly away. As she walked, she continued to talk, but this time, in a low voice, because there were people around them.

"You understand, we surely should have already been in the middle of the rainy season, when the earth drinks big gulps of water to hydrate itself. But, instead, we are still waiting for the sky to burst open. The gods are abandoning us and most of the youth are leaving for the city."

While making this last pronouncement, the Old Woman scrutinized Akissi's face to see if there was a reaction. But she remained expressionless, afraid of the crowd she sensed swarming around her, but that she could not see. When they found themselves at the heart of the market, the Old Woman stopped talking and tried to make a pathway to a seller that she knew well.

The man was seated among his animals and while he waited for clients, he was busy making a long rope. Seeing the Old Woman, he put aside his task and greeted her with an out-pouring of warmth

The choosing of the little goat was quick. The Old Woman took Akissi's hand and, very delicately, had her touch the animal's coat. The warmth of the animal ran through Akissi's fingers. A wave of tenderness overwhelmed her. She touched the little horns, then the damp muzzle. She heard its plaintive bleating.

"Is this little goat beautiful, mother?"

"Yes", the Old Woman replied, its hairs are very white and bright.

In the days that followed, the little goat was tied to a stake in the middle of the courtyard.

In the morning, Akissi woke up to the sound of its bleating and when she felt a bit lonely during the day, she went to where it was and caressed it. Sometimes, she gave it pieces of food. She became accustomed to its presence and talked to it in a soft, child-like voice as if it could understand what she was saying.

At night-fall, when the entire village seemed plunged in an atmosphere of togetherness, the Old Woman recounted to

Akissi the myths and legends of her people. She smoked her pipe and closed her eyes so as to better concentrate:

"A long, long time ago, the Mask did not exist.

Way back then, in the area, there was a woman whose mother had just died. Her pain was so great that she refused to bury her mother without having paid homage to her beforehand, by dancing around her corpse. She wanted this dance to be the most beautiful that she had ever danced.

So she started to weave a cloth made from red fibers.

When she had finished, she wrapped it around herself and started to dance. She danced and sang around her mother's corpse for three days and three nights and when finally her strength was exhausted, she lay down on the ground and went to sleep.

It was then that some men who had heard the sound of the dance came to look around. Seeing the beauty of the costume she wore, they decided to steal it. In silence, they undressed the woman and ran off with the red costume. Then, in the middle of the night, they carved a mask and hid it far away from the village, in the sacred woods.

And it is this Mask, one hundred generations old, that we still worship today.

The Mask is a source of life.
The Mask is fire.
The Mask is pure air.
When the Mask dances, no one should talk to him.
The sound of his voice is like the neigh of a wild horse.
The Mask is terrifying.
The Mask is not of this world.
No one dares pronounce his name.
The Mask can see the dead.
The songs of the Mask are ritual songs.
Listen closely to these songs.
The Mask is powerful.
Red,
Very powerful"

Chapter 18

With an Open Heart

Akissi in due course gave her heart to people in the village. The voice of the Old Woman had pierced her consciousness and had urged her to communicate with those around her. She told them about the other life, the other way of living that made her run away from her origins.

"And yet," she told them, "you shouldn't have to leave the city in order to live better. You must simply make the city more welcoming, less selfish. You must stop it from taking everything, from seizing everything to the point of destroying itself."

For days and nights, the villagers would sometimes sit around Akissi and listen to her speak like one would listen to a good storyteller. She explained to them what palace life was like with its courtesans; its betrayals; and the display of blindness. She explained the impossibility of speaking the truth; she explained the absolute power held by the king; she explained the injustice.

Akissi told them every thing that she knew, because she wanted to share; wanted to have them understand that the BlindPeople were powerful, but not invincible, weakened by indifference and greed.

Akissi had the impression of washing away all of her past wrong-doings, even if she knew that was impossible. She spoke to the villagers with an open heart. She told them that she would never ever live as she had once before.

Chapter 19

The Very Same Day

The very same day the Mask came out, Akissi's heart was beating fast when she woke up. She felt something warm running between her legs. She touched it. Her fingers were damp, covered with thick blood.

"Mother, she cried out, panicked, I'm bleeding!"

The Old Woman woke up suddenly from her sleep and turned around towards her.

"What are you saying?"

"I'm saying that I am bleeding!"

"Pssth. How unfortunate!" The Old Woman said, catching her breath.

"What are we going to do?" Akissi asked after a while.

"There is nothing to do, my daughter ... You'll have to go into isolation."

The Old Woman approached Akissi and took her hand.

"Women who are bleeding", she told her with weariness in her voice, "must leave the village before the Mask comes out. I have explained to you why this is. And so it is. Outside the village, a small hut has been constructed. It is in there that they must await his departure."

Akissi remained in a state of disbelief for several seconds, but when she understood the importance of the Old Woman's words and pronouncements, she felt like crying.

The Old Woman's heart was heavy, too. She looked for words that could ease the young woman's pain, but they didn't come. She just kept repeating to her:

"Remember, my daughter, that it was a woman who created the Mask's clothing !"

The Old Woman led Akissi up to the small hut. There, she met several women who had gotten ready to spend the night. It was a precarious shelter that collapsed during every rainy season, but was hurriedly rebuilt as soon as the weather permitted.

During the three long days that followed the coming-out of the Mask, the women talked very little among themselves. They tried to hear in the distance the beating of the tom-tom that accompanied the Mask. The village seemed far away, cut off from the rest of the world by the trees in the forest. Akissi wanted to run away. She wanted to stop everything.

But the mother knew how to calm her anxiousness. Every day, she took care of her. She washed her and she helped her clean herself. When she touched the young girl's body, it was with slow, soft movements. After a while, Akissi resisted no longer and gave in to her helping hands.

On the morning of the fourth day, the Old Woman brought her daughter back to the village.

When they got home, Akissi sensed that the courtyard was much calmer than usual. A sensation of emptiness overtook her.

"Mother, where is my little goat?"

"Be glad, my daughter", the Old Woman replied warmly, "the Elders have accepted your sacrifice. The Mask has accepted your little goat. This is a sign of good fortune to come!"

That night, Akissi's sleep was restless. She tossed, fidgeted, and turned on her mat.

The Old Woman worried about it, but decided to do nothing. Finally, at the first break of day, as Akissi awakened, she went to her and whispered:

"My child, my child, what are you afraid of?"

Hearing this familiar voice, Akissi half-smiled, then recounted her dream:

"It was night. I was alone in the middle of a path. I was scared because I did not know where I was and how I was going to find my way without someone's help. Suddenly, I heard shouting that seemed to be coming from far away. I could not understand what this meant and yet I was sure that the person who cried out was talking to me.

After several minutes, the shouting stopped and I distinctly heard the beating of a tom-tom in rhythmic movement with the neighing voice of the Mask. I then understood that the initiates were coming in my direction. But I could not move. Every part of my body was paralyzed. I realised that I could not stay there, because within seconds, I was going to be facing the Mask.

This is when a wave of energy ran through me and I started to run not knowing in which direction to go. I stumbled several times and got up, but still the tom-tom continued to resonate in my head.

Then, I don't know how this happened, but I found myself in a crowd. My hands were tied behind my back and someone pulled me by my left arm. It was at day break because I could feel faint sun rays on my skin. The crowd yelled. Bodies were pressed up against me, jostling me around and making me lose my balance. I thought that I was going to die."

At this point in her story, Akissi stopped. She shivered despite the heat. The Old Woman moved her hand softly across Akissi's forehead to wipe away the sweat. "Continue," she murmured.

Akissi went on ... "I heard a strong, deep voice that rose above the others. It was a man who spoke to the crowd. Everyone stood still and there was silence again. Then, the man started to untie me. When he had finished, he put his hand on my shoulder and declared loudly: "Let her go, she is one of us!"

The Old Woman looked at Akissi with a strange gleam in her eyes.

"Is that all?" She asked with eagerness.

"Yes, that is all, mother. After that, I do not remember anything."

"Well ..., well, it means that you are ready!" the Old Woman exclaimed laughing and squeezing Akissi's arm. "I am going to ask the Elders permission to begin the rituals."

As she did every morning, Akissi turned on her radio. The reception was not good. She put the radio next to her ear and listened attentively. It was Council meeting day.

"Buzz...buzz....crrrrrrr... we have just received an official communiqué announcing that the Council meeting that was due to take place at the palace this morning has been postponed until further notice.

We learned, from an unofficial source, that an attempt to destabilize the kingdom orchestrated by a small group of people led by the secretary of His Majesty Ato IV has been thwarted. Security forces have proceeded immediately to make a series of arrests within palace quarters. It appeared that ... crr

crrrrrr... ... ..."

Silence.

Prolonged silence.

Then no more sound. Akissi started to shake the radio furiously and press all of the buttons at once.

Several minutes later, the radio played some military music. It was as if Akissi had just been stabbed.

She would have wanted to leave right away. There. Now. She would have wanted to run to Karim. But she knew she would have to wait several days before any transport came to the village. She cried out of fear and frustration.

Chapter 20

Waiting

"Waiting, forever waiting.

Waiting for things to be resolved, for the situation to improve. Waiting for the rain to fall, for seeds to sprout, for the millet to grow and hunger to go away.

Waiting for the Others to understand; those People who are in need of nothing, who talk with their mouths full and belch in public; those People whose lips spurt vulgarities and vomit-words in the ears of the dispossessed.

Speeches and words. Words, words nothing but words. Over and over again, all the time repeating. Listening to nothing. Hearing nothing of the whispering voices saying: life is rotten and the future dead.

The king's sayings are like bloody claws that dig deep into the flesh and wound like razor blades. They cloud the vision. They blind the gaze.

Evil fetishes, foul-smelling perfumes and the king's sayings haunt the land.

Lies drawn out over years of not knowing and waiting.

Waiting, forever waiting.

Letting supernatural powers decide. Letting men with clown faces dance and play like laughing hyenas while other men with raised fingers condemn the truth-sayers.

Waiting kills slowly like a secret poison. It digs deep, gnaws, destroys the insides and what is left is a hollow corpse.

Waiting paralyzes, disfigures and saps energy. It can stomp out a life. It can annihilate a people.

Action!

Give me conscience. Give me impatience. Give me open eyes and strong muscles. Let my spirit be in motion. Let me initiate change.

I don't want this inaction. Pain binds my reasoning. Inertia erases my presence.

I've had enough of this defeated spirit, enough of people losing their tomorrow?!

Action!

Give me the courage to combat fear. Let outrage melt this lethargy. Let the shouting bring down the walls of indifference.

Waiting is like a long illness."

Chapter 21

The eye of the mask

The old man with eyes as big as the clouds; the old man with eyes like the sun, sat down facing Akissi and placed his hands on her forehead.

Next to them, the Old Woman jingled small ritual-bells as he recited sacred words in a guttural monotone:

"The eye of the Mask
Is an eye of sun
The eye of the Mask
Is an eye of fire
The eye of the Mask
Is an eye of river
Is an eye of leopard
Is an eye of land
Is an eye of spear
Is an eye of truth."

The old man with energy-bearing hands crushed hot yellow peppers and very red pepper seeds into a clay bowl. He mixed them into a paste. Then, he pounded it, he kneaded it, he flattened it out until its perfume seeped through and spread throughout the air.

He called out to the spirit of the Mask. He called out to all of the invisible ancestors who peopled the sacred forest. He called out to the founders of the village, the ancestral guardians of secrets.

Akissi kept still. When the Old Woman took her by the hand and guided her to the ritual- house, obediently, she let herself go.

Softly, slowly the Old Woman covered the young woman's body with the perfumed pepper-paste. Tingling feelings ran all over her skin in every direction. She had the impression of being attacked by a swarm of bees. Hundred of bee-stingers penetrated her skin and reduced her into boiling hot liquid. "Be brave," the Old Woman whispered, "it will go away."

Then, she took a string of coral beads and put it around Akissi's hips. She also gave her a black loin-cloth and slipped an amulet around her neck. Finally, she looked at her and determined that she was ready.

The old man with great power, started to recite incantations in his earth tongue and spat into a clay pot filled with water. He repeated *ad infinitum* incomprehensible words and when the water had drunk every word, he approached Akissi. Tipping her head back, he put water into the palm of his hands and washed her face. He washed her eye-brows, her eye-lids and eye-lashes. He put drops of water into each of her eyes.

The old man with the voice like rain sang magical lyrics, words that opened up your eyes to the entire world and way beyond. Words that lent piercing vision and clear reasoning. And his voice was as hot as larva and it burned Akissi's soul anew.

> "The Mask is power
> The Mask is consciousness
> When the moment comes
> All the world sees it
> The men see it
> The women see it
> The children see it
> The animals see it
> The people in the bush see it
> The dead see it
> If you want to
> You, too
> You can see it."

Chapter 22

The Strength To Believe

"I am giving you the strength to believe. Always keep this amulet around your neck. We, the people of the earth, are giving to you the strength to believe. You will know how to walk in the city protected by our knowledge and you will be conscious of the fact that many people are behind you. Do not be afraid. Our powers are deeply embedded like the roots of our most powerful trees. They are nourished by the flesh of the earth and draw power from her blood. Listen to the earth breathe in her own hot breath.

I, the sorcerer, the man with clay hands and a red heart, I command you to get impregnated by a man who will know how to reconcile concrete and earth; a man whose soul will feed on the soil and on ideas; a man who will come to see many things at once, from on high and from below; see the yeas and the nays, the past and the present. A man who will know how to re-think our traditions without negating them; how to understand the world without becoming alienated. Come together with this man and allow him to plant his seeds inside your belly, because it is you who will carry the great hope: a new generation who will set energy free, open closed doors and create new paths.

Come together with this man. Your union will be magic and miracle, a pagan and sacred ritual."

Chapter 23

The March

The village was heading in Karim's direction. Everyone was getting ready to rally other villages along the way. Their numbers were going to swell. People took along their *gris-gris*; amulets; and charms. The initiated walked in front: chasing away the bad spirits along the path; cursing the bearers of evil; saying words of strength and endurance. They walked on dirt roads, across tall grass and then onto paved highways. They were going to start in the morning, and even if it took several days to reach the heart of the city, when they got there, they were going to plant revolt.

They intended to consult the ancestors and dig up their powers. They were ready to go to the end, those people who had never before had anything to do with the city, until she ate up their children and ignored their distress.

Together with the slum-dwellers, they planned to unravel the city's secrets and make the BlindPeople vulnerable.

The initiated were prepared to walk in front: chasing away the bad spirits along their path; cursing the bearers of misfortune; pronouncing words of strength and endurance.

Chapter 24

Bursts of Light

The prophet says:

Light is clothed in a robe that is sometimes silk, sometimes powder. She puts on rainbow jewels. Sometimes, she dances on water and draws arabesques that move to the sound of water. Clouds move softly in and out, as bursts of diamonds, merging into the tide.

Even when the sun-rays disappear, you will remember them. The stars will roam the evening's vault and, in turn, the moon will change its smile.

When you open your eyes, the night will have gone from behind your eyelids and fear will have left you peacefully.

The fields will be cultivated and crops will ripen under a fluorescent light.

The soil will be very black and very rich and its smell will be sweet and haunting.

The city will also be cured of its woes. She will purify herself, become more beautiful and even more maternal.

She will open her arms and be:

Refuge-City
Lover-City
Beloved-City
Fertile-City.

Chapter 25

The Old Woman's Tirade

"My child, hear well and understand the call of blood.

Hear well and understand what it tells you. Times have changed and you will need convictions.

This bird that cries out a strange agonizing sound in the night is my restless spirit.

It is my soul erasing itself because I already know that I am breathing in the dust of centuries.

Memory is our most precious gift. With it we can conquer time that traps us. You must remember everything that I have told you and still many other things so that this city in ruins and dying villages can rebuild themselves. Hold on dearly to the knowledge from the earth and give it new forms.

Thereafter, you will be able to erect huge buildings that reach all the way to the sky and you will be able to search for what makes life easier and less backbreaking.

My daughter, your body is made to carry children. How could I ask you to be like me who has reached the end of the road?

Go, life will know how to make you cry from joy and from pain. Go, be careful, because there will always be someone to try to imprison your will.

Go, there are many ways of dying and the hardest is not the one you are thinking of. As for me, I want to slide slowly under the earth and take on my initial form once again.

Tomorrow, when the sun rises, you will be different, because

64

you will see life such as it is, because you will know from whence you come.

I am telling you all of this now because my death is approaching. It will not be my tired body that will kill me; it will be this violence that is unleashing itself inside me and breaking my bones. It has come to be that my nights are so very long...

My daughter, never lose sight of your own self image, the one that lines the walls of your spirit and pushes you to think that you are on the right road.

Do not squander your soul, and if one day you must die, let it be after you have given your life to stop the end of the world."

Part
Four

Chapter 26

Darkness and Light

The morning seeped through the small window of the round-house. Akissi opened her eyes, soaked up the light and looked around. She saw the beaten soil. She saw the clay pots. She saw the tobacco leaves that dried on a cord. And then her gaze steadied on the Old Woman who slept, with her back turned towards her, huddled in the fetal position. She let out a cry of joy that filled her body with a delightful shiver.

At the same moment, very far away from her, Karim was trying to avoid despair. Crouched down in his dark cell, he suffocated from heat. An acrid stench hurt his nostrils and made him nauseous.

Around him, nothing. Nothing but four walls. Puddles of urine yellowed the ground. Coiled up, his body had become burned. His eyes remained open in the darkness, refusing to allow for even a second of rest.

He had not eaten anything since he was put in prison. He did not want a single bite of their food. What obsessed him more than anything else was the filth that covered everything.

On that day, the guards had let him go out for a few minutes into the court yard to empty his waste bucket. He had taken advantage of it to observe what was happening around him. The camp was vast. Everywhere there were cells like his. The doors were all bolted. Where were his comrades? What had happened to them? He would have wanted to question the guards but their faces were sculpted in stone.

In the middle of the night, Karim heard cries, howling that escaped from neighboring cells. Rapid footsteps and outbursts across the courtyard. He remained on his mat in a corner, unable to believe what was happening.

All of a sudden, the heavy iron door burst open. An armed man appeared in the doorway. He took a piece of string from his pocket and tied up Karim's hands.

Outdoors, the sky was starless. Not the faintest breeze of wind blew. They walked to a building at the far end of the prison camp.

The guard opened a door and violently pushed him into a room that oddly resembled a classroom. There was a desk of sorts installed next to the back wall, with several chairs arranged in front of it.

After a fifteen minute wait, a group of men erupted into the room. Karim recognized them immediately: they were the main members of the Council, with the Minister of Armies in front.

"So, Secretary, you want to dethrone our good king Ato IV, now?" the minister shouted as he came towards him.

Karim shot back at him a contemptuous look. Facing him was the most feared man of the kingdom, one of the rare members of the OtherPeople in whom the king placed total confidence. His face was swollen by alcohol and his eyes were blood-shot. The hatred that was in him was stronger than anything else, as if having betrayed his own people had triggered a murderous insanity.

"Have you lost your tongue?! Trying to be clever won't help you here!"

"Why am I in this prison camp? What does all of this mean?" Karim, ignoring the Minister's question, addressed the council members instead.

"Shut up!" the Minister hurled, "you are not at the palace anymore! You and your gang, think that you can get away with murder. You think that you are above everybody; above the royal court and above the people, too. But the truth is, you are nothing, just pitiful saboteurs ready to plunge the kingdom into chaos!"

"You have lost your damned mind, haven't you?"

In response, the Minister punched the wind out of Karim, leaving him breathless for several minutes. Karim tried to defend himself, but his hands were tied up so he was powerless.

"Ah! You think you talk in the name of the people, huh? Well, no! You stand for nothing and no one. You are only flies on the walls and we are going to crush the life out of you. All of you! In your opinion, what would the people do if we let you have your little revolution? You will be the first to feel the heat. Imbecile! What do you think? Surely you don't believe that these bare-feet would be content with your weak reforms, do you! No, if we let you do what you want, they would crush our bones like wild beasts. And then, they would take our places and destroy the kingdom!"

"You have lost your mind completely!"

A second punch made him lose his balance. Karim wanted to resist, but a kick landed him on the ground. After a sign given by the Minister, the body guards joined in the action and very quickly all of them attacked him like wild dogs. Karim started to shout, yell, scream, because he knew very well that was what they wanted. Hearing the cries, the Blind Counselors stomped with enthusiasm and raised their fists in the air.

Karim lost his strength. The body guards hoisted him up by the arms and put him in a chair. The Minister of Armies bent down towards him and whispered, angrily clenching his teeth:

"Okay. Good. You will talk, now, won't you, Secretary? You will tell us everything about your organization. Absolutely everything. Isn't that right?"

Chapter 27

Karim's Memories

In the blazing heat of his stinking cell, Karim remembered his childhood.

Back then, he wasn't afraid of anything, since he did not know that, one day, he was going to die. The scent of the earth was the only truth he possessed. The days followed lined up in single file, one after the other. When the evening came, he would say, in a low voice, words that had withstood the test of time, words that his mother had taught him: "Let the sun rise on a clear day! Let the rains fall on to the fields."

And yet, the gods were not always generous. Often, the full heat of the sun bore down, breaking the backs of peasants and drying out the soil, making it as hard as a rock. These seasons were difficult. Hunger lived in their stomachs. The entire village was plunged into silence.

What he remembered most, however, were the rainy days when the sky exploded and water bathed the earth, washing away the tiredness and quenching the soil's thirst. Then, rivers were swollen, vegetation turned green and the village was born again.

Yet over the years, he had come to understand he would have to leave. Go further away. It wasn't just because of all he had learned, but because of a pervasive feeling he could not resist. He had the impression that his life was not his alone; that he had to make an offering of it to others so it could end that dependence on the gods, the sun, the rain and on the earth.

Then, one day, this feeling turned into a certainty. He had convinced himself that he had to go over there, to the city, in order to save his village that was dying a slow death, giving way to its own fate.

He knew, from that point on, that he was not one of those people prepared to accept destiny sitting down nor a person who left it to time to make things happen. He knew that in the big city, there was power. And he wanted to get close to that power, so he could liberate his village from slavery. That was his obsession, his main wish and it was embedded deep into his skin. It guided his every footstep and every decision, robbing him of the carefree life of youth, and turning him into some kind of spokesperson.

But when he got to the city, the days, the months, the years took hold of him. The king monopolized power, imposed his every will, and controled the life of his subjects. So, Karim's sleep became peopled with fears: Power was going to swallow him up, steal his soul and destroy the only thing, the only reason that had brought him into the palace. Ministers, like hyenas, turned round and round him, sniffed his thoughts, wrecked all of his projects.

One night, he awoke suddenly from one of his many nightmares, and screamed: "No, you will not have my soul! You will not have my voice!" Then secretly, he left to join the slum-dwellers.

With them, everything would change, he told himself, and he knew that he would never rest as long as this desire echoed in his head. He realized that saving his own village would not be enough, he also had to fight for other villages, and against other injustices.

And yet, in the palace, he met some like-minded people who shared the same generous spirit as him and whose hearts were filled with hope. The darkness of the palace had not succeeded in upholding the image they had made of the world. They knew all too well what they expected from life. Like him, they thought it was possible to bring on change through persuasion and underground struggles. In truth, they did not realize how evil the courtesans' blindness was.

They believed that nothing was static and that everything could be resolved one day. They wanted to give people another chance as they were persuaded that, in the end, justice would prevail. All they needed to do was to explain, convince, find the right words even if, in the beginning, no one listened to them. Even if some people tried to silence their voices.

They promised each other they would do all they could so that one day there would be no North, no South, no East nor West- only one and the same country visited by hope.

"But where was the fire they needed to make their words burn deep?" Karim asked himself. "Where was the strength they needed to give to their words some cutting edge, the power of weapons?"

Chapter 28

Sleeping/Karim's near despair

Sleeping with all of his might. Sleeping to remember nothing. Sleeping to forget everything. Sleeping for as long as possible. Closing his eyes and behind his eyelids he recreated a liquid world of no weights nor measures, no joy nor pain.

Sleeping inside a timeless void, body stretched out, vanishing, as if in total bliss and hardly discernable, the slight purring from his lungs. No movement. His face smooth, wiped of all frustration.

Sleeping and sleeping, days upon end, nights turning into mornings, the sun melting like butter. Far away from everything. Much closer to the beats of the heart. Swimming, bringing back to the blurred surface, the calm of dissolution. With no dreams or nightmares.

As in days long ago, sleeping without reopening his eyes again, lulled by the never ending dissolution of movement. The perpetual fusion of gestures. Being nothing but a low sigh. At long last, the relaxation of every pent-up muscle whether paralyzed or deadened by the passing years.

Sleeping until satiated, so as to obscure the pain of living. To fall into the silence of bottomless seas.

After the sound and the rage. After rebelling, after yelling at the top of his lungs, with the fury of a mad drummer. After telling some truths and denouncing the same mistakes that had been made hundreds and hundred of times. After exhausting himself to find a meaning to his life.

He was born in a warm ocean, in water that echoed to the sound of a voice, and to the sound of a heart beating close to his head.

Inside the warmth of a body, shriveled in darkness, listening to his mother live, mixing into her for an eternity.

Inside this nurturing water, floating, eyes closed by a night with no day, by one long night that after all wasn't one since it had neither fear nor desire.

He was inside her. Body inside body. Forever floating inside an unfathomable sleep.

Sleeping, at a stretch, unbelievably well.

Chapter 29

The Descent into Hell

The car swallowed up the last kilometers in big gulps. The city was getting closer. The heat was burning. The carcasses of animals lay strewn, charred by the sunlight. A dying dog on the sidewalk pawed the air. Oxygen was thin. Sweat soaked skin. It seemed there was no shade and that never again would there be coolness, freshness.

Akissi suffocated. She believed that the space had shrunk and that soon they would be caught in flames.

Suddenly, an eagle tore across the sky, its black wings wide open, soaring above the desolate landscape. There was something very pure about this quiet flight. Akissi thought: "Misery and chaos don't pollute the sky. We, we must struggle alone in a filthy world." And this image of the bird, pinned against the sunlight, remained imprinted on her memory as a dark sun.

The trees were drying up. And the soil cracking open before your eyes. You needed to run away instead of moving forward. To leave this place where the air was too scorching and where the clouds couldn't have cared less.

As they got to the city gate, the hills looked like the coat of a mangy, grayish, brown dirty dog. The plants there had sprouted with thorns. Akissi thought: "I would sell my soul for a little fresh air."

She questioned: "Could it be that we have been abandoned?"

They arrived in one of the city slums where an atmosphere of chaos reigned. It looked like a bomb site. As if the sky had crashed down at this very place. Everything was lifeless and grief-stricken. Misery was imprinted on people's face.

They came upon a gathering and Akissi asked: "What's going on over there?" Someone responded: "It's the poet, prophet, fool, storyteller, the wise-one who is speaking." Moving closer, they observed that the people were crowded around a man who made sweeping gestures and who spoke in a high pitched voice:

"There are people who seek the truth at the risk of losing their lives. Their eyes are wide open and they know how to see well beyond the horizon. They seek hidden truth; tried and tested truth; truth from yesterday. So they can understand tomorrow and tame it.

But who has said that truth would be easy to find? I repeat who has said that this truth would be easy to find?"

Akissi had the impression that at this precise moment, the prophet was addressing her. Her heart started to beat wildly.

Then he looked around the whole crowd to be assured he had their full attention. Satisfied, he started his tirade with an even greater passion.

"Bad luck has struck us! Bad luck has struck us! Dry your tears! Now, is the time to get on the right path. It won't be easy to carry our inadequacies while searching for a meaning in the way time elapses. But we must keep going. We must resist. We must reverse our roles and create a new life. Don't talk to me about utopia. Don't talk to me about being a dreamer. Don't talk to me about fantasies! All of us are striving to find a balance in this hostile world.

Listen! Bad luck will strike again and history's twists and turns will be numerous, but in the end we will succeed in imprisoning injustice! We must have courage. We must dissent!

Rise up!

Dry your tears, dry your tears!

Advance, you who carry courage

Approach, you who tame life!

Come, you who have nerves of steel!

We need

Hopeful Warriors!

78

Chapter 30
The Tidal Wave

According to a bystander, the rally started at 12 o'clock sharp. Polluted clouds weighed heavily over the entire city. The air was muggy.

The tight mass of slum-dwellers descended the hills like a tidal wave or a downpour of lava. Cries fired the sky and fists cut through the overheated atmosphere: FREE KARIM! FREE THE PRISONERS!" The men tapped empty cans to give more weight to the words they shouted. The women yelled and the children clapped their hands.

Except for this fury of sound, the crowd walked non-violently, shaking off the dread and carrying within an intense force.

The goal was to cross the entire city and get to the palace.

They had already reached the avenue that led to the beautiful neighborhoods when army trucks sped ahead and cut off the route. Soldiers got out and formed a roadblock. Seeing them like that ... planted to the ground, stiff as sycamores, helmets squeezed between their ears, shiny leather boots, and hands on their guns ... the children started to shout insults: "Cockroaches! Stinking Bats! Traitors! "

At this precise moment, the bystander's recollection became somewhat blurred. He could no longer remember whether the gunfire started before or after people started to throw rocks at the soldiers. Whatever the case, within seconds, it was horror! Bullets were whizzing on all sides of the crowd, panic struck and people jostled as they tried to get away. Many were shot in the back. Men, women and children fell one on top of the other. Frightful cries were mingled with the thunder of submachine gunfire.

When the soldiers ceased firing, the avenue was strewn with cadavers. They piled the corpses into their trucks and took off at full speed.

Chapter 31

The Last Embrace

Akissi mounted the grand staircase which was covered with bat waste.

After a long hesitation, the soldiers recognized her and let her pass, not noticing that she had changed.

That day, for the daughter of the king, reality revealed itself and it was horrible. The dirt and stench of the palace made her nauseous. She had to gather up her strength to continue moving forward.

Inside, everything was a cacophony of colors, forms and fabrics. Dust and grime had taken over. Looking haggard, several courtesans dragged their feet from one room to the next.

When she opened the door of the royal chamber, Akissi laid eyes on her father, for the first time in her life. She felt a sharp pain in her heart.

This man was finished. He was asleep in a wide armchair upholstered in thick velvet. His head rested on the back of the chair. His mouth was open and raucous snores escaped from his mouth. A thin line of saliva streamed from his lips. His skin was dry. His hair and his beard looked dirty.

She did not dare approach him. She did not dare awaken him. She would have liked to turn around, but that was not possible; she had to talk with him.

Karim's eyes were sad, despite his smile expressing a desire to keep hoping. Two folds marked his forehead like a tattoo, etching on his face the suffering he had endured. His body, with its drooped shoulders and weak limbs, seemed drained. But Akissi knew it was not physical fatigue that assaulted him, right now; rather, it was weariness that comes from the heart and soul when the world all around you turns into a labyrinth.

However, she still loved his face passionately because it was like the one she had dreamed about. A face deprived of lies, of pretence. She wanted to give back to this man the desire to live, to find a solution to free him from this ordeal he didn't deserve.

But Karim harbored no illusions. His long days in detention made him understand the immensity of his mistake. Never would the courtesans accept to change their way of life. For them, it was stagnation, paralysis, keeping the status quo. They had too much to lose, and they were prepared to do anything to protect their privileges. As soon as they sensed that someone had threatened their power, they resorted to violence. And to think that in his incredible naivety he had believed it was possible to reverse the course of things! He would have to pay heavily for this delusion.

Akissi declared:

"Listen, the king is ready to free you immediately, if you repent in public. The kingdom is in a state of total upheaval. He wants to restore calm."

She had said all of this in a single breath, fearing he would cut her off. Her heart beat rapidly and boiling blood rushed through her veins and her hands were moist and hot. Karim was staring at emptiness. Inside his eyes, she saw a mirroring of bad omens.

She wanted to challenge him, to cry out her fear of losing him, but all she could do was reach out her hand to touch him.

Because words had become useless, now. Because communication had become impossible. The world was adrift. How could she explain the extent of her own despair?

Akissi closed her eyes. A sharp pain dug its claws into her flesh. Everything had been said. She knew it. And how could it have been otherwise? It was despair that had dictated her words. Deep down, she had always known he would refuse.

So, Akissi spent three days and three nights next to Karim. And after these three days and these three nights, they got to know each other, again. They found their tender feelings again, and the complicity that had united them. During these three days and these three nights, they recreated the world one more time. They took stock of their mistakes and of their victories. But it was about their mistakes they talked especially. What had they made of their destiny? Weren't they mere puppets looking for solutions that they didn't have?

"Maybe," Akissi said, "had I not been so hampered by inaction, by an incapacity to be committed to anything, we would have succeeded."

"Maybe," Karim said, "had I known how to understand history, I would have acted in a different way. Life is not written in black and white. I underestimated the various forces, burned too many bridges, bypassed reasoning, neglected true analyses."

"Perhaps you should have loved a woman other than me. I have no convictions. I let go of everything very quickly. I can't stand suffering. For each step forward I take one backwards. I lack courage. I give in to life. My greatest passions come from love. I saw that in you a different kind of flame was burning and I wanted to get to it. But, already, my wings had been burned by your ardor. Already, I know I will never have your strength and your endurance.

"Don't idealize me," Karim responded. "Don't see me as larger than life. That makes me weak. That makes me lose my head. I am no better than anyone else. The love I feel for my country is not enough to excuse my faults. I will always blame myself for having not revolted sooner; for having taken such a long time to understand what had to be changed. For too long, I pushed back the moment of plunging into the crowd. If today, I speak of liberation, how many times have I betrayed it? If today, I speak of justice how many times have I not let injustice be? What right did I have to go so wrong?

I'm disappointed. I'm weary. I'm at the end of the rope for hoping"

So, Akissi caressed his face and whispered:

"You must not give up hope. We will start all over again. With more experience and vision. We will take into account how strange and complex this world is. From then on we will dismiss easy symbols and simplistic ideas. We will know how to deal with reality.

But for now, we must accept defeat and learn how to survive."

Now that destiny had taken charge of their life, there was only the two of them and their love took a different direction. From that point on, they no longer searched for the indissoluble union of lovers who, beyond time, try to attain eternity. From that point on, they didn't have a future anymore. No promises to keep. No more rendezvous.

So, like two humans meeting each other for the last time, inside this small, dark prison where no semblance of hope could survive, they decided to draw a line through everything and find again the only truth they still possessed: that of their love.

And their gestures were animated by an unknowable passion. They made love, found each other again, conquered the despair that devoured them. Going and coming, they held on to each other like two shipwrecks tossed around by life.

Chapter 32

Karim's monologue after Akissi's departure

Karim felt lost. Solitude was glued to his skin. It was a night of dangerous insomnia. A night that killed his strength and stole his energy.

"What will we become in this kingdom that's breaking down, falling apart and splattering? In this country where soon violence will be running in the streets and fire will be climbing the trees. What are we going to do in this kingdom where rage is written on the clouds and stones are thrown all the way to the sky. What are we going to do when we can no longer demonstrate or think and are lost in the chaos?

What will we become in this kingdom where everything is unsettled, where it is impossible to live one's life and where souls are slowly rotting?

Must we uproot the country?

Already, I see that time is moving faster than all of us. The choices that remain are disappearing with each passing day. How can we forget that this kingdom leaves no place for people, it locks and traps them in a place where they fight and scratch and kill each other.

But, how can we not suffer from the wounds of this city that oozes with despair? How can we not lose our minds inside this black hole where the spirit is dismantling? Hell exists. Misery is our mortal sin, our deep cancerous wound.

What are we going to do, Akissi?

What are we going to do to give our love, a chance to survive, a chance in this evil city?

It's so difficult to live away from you. To be unable to touch you again and again until peace comes back. To be unable to fall asleep by your side, to construct another world, to create another language.

Akissi, that would be crazy ... you know this ... to expect everything from one another. I know why you have come to see me. You can not keep anything secret from me. You are feeling lonely. You want me to help your life. But can't you see that solitude is my most loyal companion? Don't you understand that I can never live your life for you?

With me, you are in danger. I am addicted to a passion that is stronger than anything else. If you stay with me, I will have you touching the bottom of the ocean. I will put your body to the test of fire. I will crush your illusions and turn them into mush.

What drives me, I don't know. The electricity that runs through my nerves hurts me. Struggling with all of my might, this is what consumes my energy and my will.

What will we become in this city that eats our guts? In this country where there's no oasis, no relief, no direction?

In this city that shows us its decline. In this city that dissects and devours. And the sounds of the voices of the downtrodden are drumming on our conscience, while all those whose lives are filled with misfortune and misery move and meet in the four corners of the wind. And the mud and the earth smear filth on everything that used to stand?"

Chapter 33

Akissi's Remorse

"If it is time for us to part, already, I will leave without making a sound. No longer will I try to touch your destiny. No longer will I seek to sway your decisions.

But how do you expect me to survive?

You are alone. I am alone. The city has put itself between us. We would have had to fight together. I would have won with your courage and you would have won with my hope. But we have remained separate and we have lost.

And I would not even have achieved the impossible best. Not any more than anyone else.

My love was of no use.

Still, you will see, I shall break my chain as the king's daughter. I will destroy the prison I was born into and I will plunge into the crowd of the OtherPeople.

But how do you expect me to survive with an incurable nostalgia for your presence?

How am I going to survive, since I did not get to hold your hand, get to know you, truly, and penetrate the confines of your being?

How am I going to survive, knowing I did not know where to find the words to make you renounce death, that I did not know where to find the strength to kill my father?"

Chapter 34

The Crucifixion

Shut up! interrupted the king. Guards! Guards!

The men arrived in step and stood-still before him.

"Grab my daughter!" he ordered.

They hesitated for a split second.

"Imbeciles! Do what I am telling you! And lock her up in the basement!"

Akissi was taken by the arm and forcefully led away. She struggled as much as she could but the guards held her strongly.

They made her go into an enormous room where the walls were bare. The door slammed shut, leaving her entirely alone. A small bed was in the corner against the back wall. An ivory crucifix was lying on the bed table.

Christ on the cross. Christ in the image of man, with his hands and feet nailed.

His pain was greater than the world's suffering. Which Madonna would shed tears over his death? In this indifferent city, who would share in his martyrdom?

For days. For weeks. For months. The kingdom was always in total turmoil.

The king had gone mad. He issued orders then revoked them, just minutes later. He went berserk for little or no reason. He dismissed all his cabinet members and recalled them one after the other. He insisted that everyone was to be present, but he wanted to talk to no one.

He didn't bathe anymore. He didn't change his clothes anymore. He let his beard grow. He let his hair grow. He let his fingernails grow. His breath made the people who approached him sick.

Every day, he ordered enormous quantities of food which he only ate one bite of.

On the other hand, he had many bottles of wine opened and he drank methodically until he slumped over and fell asleep on his wide table.

Fear held sway in him. He felt old. He felt threatened.

"Why now?" he asked himself over and again. "Why now, when I have lost my strength of long ago and my bones cause me to suffer? Why is this country in commotion now?"

Indeed, it was a time of endless demonstrations. Every day, the slum dwellers marched in a tight mass across the city. The repression was fierce, but each time the soldiers became a little less courageous. Doubt had infiltrated their minds. They now understood that they were struggling against the ones who resembled them the most. Many stripped off their uniforms and left for the slums. Meanwhile, the BlindPeople barricaded them-selves in their living quarters or looked for an escape.

In the palace, those who had sacrificed everything so they could get away from the slums, those who had betrayed their fathers and their mothers in order to line up along side the BlindPeople now realized that their world had fallen apart.

Those who had placed all their bets on the present and only the present, without ever having one thought for tomorrow, those who had let themselves be swept away by an ocean of lies, those who had refused to see despite their open eyes, those who had chosen to sit on the side of injustice, now felt their existence was shattered. The palace had become a prison and their elegant clothes, their heavily weighted chains, their titles, a life sentence.

And they wandered around the deserted rooms like lost spirits haunted by the memory of their treachery. They felt their time was nearing and told each other that destiny, in the end, had never let go.

The BlindPeople had already renounced them, sent them back to the far end of the palace: traitors yesterday, they would be traitors tomorrow, no doubt so they were left to suffocate in rooms where the air had thinned out.

Since they had done everything like the BlindPeople, to the point of mimicking their blindness, since they had followed close in their footsteps and had agreed to curse the future, since they had abandoned Karim and the OtherPeople, had laughed at their words and laughed at their defeat, since they had praised the king's rulings and asked for more harshness, since they had done nothing to stop the massacre of the slum dwellers, since they had refused to see in spite of their wide open eyes, they regrouped in a dark, damp and moldy smelling room. There, each man, each woman, grabbed a steel-bladed knife and slit their eyes. Ruptured cornea, perforated iris, NO EYES. Ruptured cornea, perforated iris, NO EYES.

And the world fell into a night without a morning, a deep grotto, a nightmare where feelings got lost, where time had no meaning.

Chapter 35
Akissi's Solitude

Akissi's solitude was bottomless. Each day, she descended further and further into the void. She drowned herself in the muddy waters of her nightmares and she would have wanted to end her life. But her belly was plump and round like ripe fruit. Her breasts were heavy with milk and her whole body was soft and welcoming, protector of a birth to come.

And it was the living creature within her intense solitude that helped her to survive. Karim had planted life inside her. Maybe from this life hope would be born.

Because Akissi's solitude was absolute. Without anything to gaze upon. A naked solitude, as smooth as a pebble. Between the four walls of her golden prison, she stirred up her anxiety: How would the child be at birth? How would it grow? Would she know how to teach it not to be blind?

"Going round and round in circles. We are all going round and round in circles! Always the suffering, always. Always the same mistakes. Show me something else! I say, show me something else! I didn't open my eyes to see hell. I didn't open my eyes to see destruction!

Help me! I am dying from this solitude, from this imprisonment that makes me scream.

I will be a carrier of life. I will give to this child my blood, my fluid to drink and my entire flesh to eat. On condition that it is different. On condition that the child is not born blind! Because my strength rests in this child. In the depth of my dreams, nothing else exists. Not one thing that resembles hope. I see faces, yes, many faces, but nothing that I can call hope. I lost my faith in one of those tall churches where I never should have taken part in the long and monotone ritual of pompous mass. My faith, I would have come to know it when walking bare foot, getting warm in the sun and bathing in the rain.

I lost my faith when I needed it most, when I understood that the dye was cast, when my nostrils began to smell the stench of rot mixed with the heavy vapors from rich perfumes.

Help me! The earth is getting smaller, death is getting closer! Holding you in my arms, Karim, falling asleep with you. Awakening with you. I need the fire of your presence. I need the touch of your fingers on my skin.

Karim, Karim, where are you? We no longer share the same destiny. Where we have failed, others will succeed."

Epilogue/Chapter 36
Death/Life

In the middle of the night, Karim was awakened. Without saying one word, they led him to the other side of the prison yard, to the place where hangings were held. He had awaited this moment for a long time. He simply wondered why they hadn't come sooner and why they had chosen this starry night to decide. As for himself, he had been ready for months.

He had always known that he would die this way. In secret. Under the canopy of the sky. Far away from everyone. Not even with the satisfaction of knowing that someone would weep at his grave.

"They will get rid of my body, for sure. In a place where no-one would find it. Maybe they will bury it in one of those communal graves that are discovered years later. No names on the skeletons piled one on top of the other.

It wasn't the idea of dying that caused him pain, it was the idea of dying this death, at the hands of these men.

A slight breeze carried noises from the city, Karim could not make out the ones who anticipated his death. But he was not afraid. All he had was disdain for these men who did not know that their turn would come fast and that their deaths would be much harder than his.

Theirs would be death at high noon, before a crowd howling its rage pent-up over rotten years after rotten years. Theirs would be a vengeful death.

The trap-door gave way.

Karim dropped down.

Muscles stiffened. His blood-shot eyes bulged. His body tightened.

Akissi's contractions came closer and closer together. Stronger and stronger. To her it seemed that her insides were about to split open and her entrails were going to be torn away by the force that was pushing.

Outside, the slum-dwellers had begun the siege of the palace. They came like an angry mass that no guard had dared to confront. Only the heavy bolted doors of the palace blocked their move forward.

Eagles drew huge circles in the sky, their powerful wings cutting the air like bolts of lightening. All of a sudden, they would swoop down into the trees and stick their claws into the skin of the bats. Then, they flew off carrying their prey. While kite-flying, they unlocked their grip leaving the bats to crash, like overly ripened fruit, onto the arid ground.

The madman, the prophet, the wise poet was in the crowd perched on the top of the grand staircase. He spoke very loudly and gestured incessantly. He proclaimed:

"The lives of some people we can not comprehend. Fate is not to be explained. Everything happens as if there were two parallel worlds with nothing in between.

I invite you to hope, to share the pain of suffering together. Nothing is possible without sacrifice. You must be ready to offer your soul as sustenance and to give freely of your bodies without keeping count. I invite you to hope. Hope like a flash of lightning that breaks up in the distance. I speak of a light in the dusk. "

A few feet away from the prophet, a group of children were having fun dissecting the bats and looking at their guts. Several women, with their heads turned around and with their eyes riveted on the sun, sang a song of war and peace.

Soon thereafter, not a single bat remained. There were only the eagles performing a strange ballet in the middle of the sky. And like shooting stars, their shadows cast onto the earth strange messages and furtive signs. It was as if the world had turned itself upside down. As if the laws of nature had become something else. With all its force, the crowd pushed against the bolted doors of the palace.

Akissi bit her lips. She tried to fight the pain. It had hurt her so much, this pain that came from inside, from a hidden place in her body, a place she knew nothing of, a place where life could reside, but where death could also lurk.

A long scream. And suddenly, a torrent of water poured out. And with the water, came the blood. And with the blood came a head, a face, a wrinkled and shriveled body, moist and covered with blood.

Then, Akissi's womb started to contract again. Just as strong. Once again. And then water poured. And more blood spilled. And another head appeared, another face, another wrinkled and shriveled body, moist and covered with blood.

Now, it was over. Akissi had forgotten the pain. Akissi started to laugh. Bursts of laughter and joy. There, on the blood-soaked floor, a girl and a boy cried at the top of their voices.

* * *

An Interview with Véronique Tadjo
by Janis A. Mayes

" ... 3 Black Women, working on all sides of the Atlantic and sides of the Book, have made this happen, a historic moment in itself."

Best to us,
Janis A. Mayes

JAM: We open the book and are faced immediately with a vivid image of a catastrophic earthquake. There is devastation everywhere. Where does this image come from? Did you have a particular place or happening in mind here?

VT: Prior to the writing of the book, I lived in Mexico City for several months. It was around 1986, right after the big earthquake that destroyed part of the city. You could still see the ruins of many buildings and there were constant references to the earthquake in the news. Later on, when I started to work on the novel, l needed an image which could express the type of devastation that can shake the foundations of a country, a people. The Mexican earthquake came to my mind. I used it as a metaphor of colonization and the traumatizing effects it had on African societies as a whole. It destroyed the fabric of African life. Already before that, the Atlantic Slave Trade had turned the world upside down for Africans. The novel starts with people trying to salvage what they could after a major earthquake. This for me is an allegory for the years of the independences (1960s) in Africa because for a short while everybody thought that there was an opportunity to turn the tide of history. But this did not happen. African leaders were not able or willing to shake off neo-colonialism. Hence, for the majority of the people, hopes for a better future were crushed. In some instances dictatorial governments were established. The BlindPeople stand for an elite blind to inequality.

JAM: Chapter 2 opens with the image of a palace, with a king and royalty ... filth is everywhere. I feel the neo-colonial in this image! Is it a reference to some of the "palaces" you find in some African countries under corrupt regimes? Isn't there also something of the Palace of Versailles' Hall of Mirrors?

VT: Absolutely. You are right to bring out the neo-colonial in this image of the palace. The rot and dirt are of course as much physical as they are mental. It is a state of affairs that is unacceptable and no amount of gold and riches can erase this. The squandering of money and the corruption that characterize the way so many heads of states rule our countries is mind-blowing. It seems like we are living in another age. The Versailles Hall of Mirrors? Yes, too many of our rulers behaved like absolute kings from centuries ago. Ahmadou Kourouma captured this craziness in his novels and Sony Labou Tansi dealt with this as well, but with a lot of derision.

JAM: For Akissi, the king's daughter and for her mother, is blindness a code for something else? Their blindness strikes me as not being a debilitating disability. Both women are seers, no? Where does their power to see and to act come from?

VT: Yes, you are right. Akissi's blindness is not a debilitating one. But don't forget that she is living in the Palace which has been custom made for the BlindPeople. In their own environment, blindness is never an issue. But through love, Akissi becomes suddenly aware of her disability and is so dissatisfied that she seeks Karim for answers. Akissi's uneasiness and inner questioning come from her rebellious mother who did not accept the status quo. But this alone is not sufficient for the two women to "see". By falling in love and associating herself with Karim, Akissi not only breaks a taboo but also initiates new possibilities. She is a strong woman in the sense that she is not afraid to seek the truth. The power to see comes from within, from the realization that injustice is unacceptable. It also comes from the desire to go towards other people. It comes from a sense of community.

JAM: Karim ... I could picture him right away ... Beautiful ... Tall, dark, handsome, a sensual kind of man, with revolutionary politics... I pictured Kwame Ture ... Stockley Carmichael! Did you have a particular person in mind, or a character which resonates beyond any one national space?

VT: I wanted him to be a real person, somebody likeable and attractive and definitively approachable. I did not want him to be a stereotype but a man of flesh and blood. He has his strong points and his weak ones, like everybody else. What interested me was to show his passionate nature because without passion you can't achieve anything. He gives himself entirely. Even though he knows by the end of the story that he has failed to achieve what he wanted to do, he is ready to die for his beliefs. It is his unshakeable faith in the future that travels through the crowd outside the gates of the Palace. It is the fuel of change. When you think of revolutionaries like Kwame Ture, Stockley Carmichael, Patrice Lumumba and even Che Guevara, for example, you see that there is something radiant in their personalities. They have an aura that pulls people towards them and this aura can also be charged with sexual energy.

JAM: Akissi, on the other hand, I had a difficult time grasping, at first ... well, even to the end. But, there are women like Akissi, right? Who is this woman?

VT: I guess we are not used to portraying women as revolutionaries. But what is a revolutionary? For me it is someone who rises above his or her circumstances and changes the status quo. You have to understand where Akissi is coming from. As you rightly pointed out, she is the king's daughter. Now, how do you overcome this and get rid of your shackles – yes, shackles? That's where the image of the blindness comes from. For me, the problem with our continent resides principally in its blind elite. The bourgeoisie could have been a factor for progress but in fact were rapacious and blind and have failed the majority of the people. If only they had looked at the long term, a lot of innovations and reforms would have happened because, it is obvious that economic and political stability is good for everybody and the precondition for development. But our elites are often far more interested in accumulating wealth and holding on to power at all costs than in doing what is often common sense. They have a short term vision that leaves little room for improvement. The consequence is that the only way of achieving change is often a violent one: military coups, rebellions and uprisings. Akissi has to dissociate herself from her class, her upbringing, and that is already a big step. She goes in search of another reality, a new truth. It would have been easy for me as a writer to "temper" Akissi's character. I could have made her this woman of steel capable of overcoming everything. But a character dictates his or her own credibility. I realized early on that she was limited in her political action because she is too attached to life to accept the violence and death that can come with revolution. However, the birth of the twins is a sign of hope, the assumption that a new generation will be born that will carry their parents' struggle forward.

JAM: What about the sexual attraction between Akissi and Karim? It seems at times that sexuality is all encompassing.

VT: Physical love serves here as a symbol of total commitment. For example, it is only by being intimate with Akissi that Karim becomes aware of the distressing emptiness in her eyes. So here and there he decides to free her from her blindness because he now feels that she is part of him. It would be a betrayal to leave her in that state. The love story is the driving force of the novel. It is through the coming together of Karim and Akissi that we realize that there is no intrinsic obstacle that prevents people of different class, gender, or ethnicity from coming together. Love has a redeeming power. I am referring here to a multi-dimensional type of love which paves the way for progress and tolerance.

JAM: To go back to Akissi's mother, what happens to her?

VT: Akissi's mother wanted to share power or rather she disagreed with the king on major issues. She tried to oppose him and bring about change. Ato IV felt challenged. Therefore, he chose to "get rid of her". We don't know if she was killed or if she was just sent away. But judging by the mystery that surrounds her one can expect the worst.

JAM: What about Karim's mother? Where does her power come from? She is portrayed as a very, very strong woman.

VT: Yes, indeed, she is strong. She is the bearer of tradition. Her power comes from the land, her culture and her community. She is also highly spiritual having been initiated into the ancestral religion. In matriarchy, power runs through women. Akissi's gift of life at the end of the story continues this. The birth of the twins may herald a new generation capable of doing better than their predecessors.

JAM: Talking of a better future, what hope is there for our cities? The city represented in *The Blind Kingdom* could be any city, any Black community where police brutality and violence take place. Pollution fills the air, and Akissi leaves in search of a better life "in the North." However, birds do manage to survive – what does their survival signal to you as a writer?

VT: I am appalled at the state of our cities, of the environment in which we live. You can have luxury residences next to shanty towns. Look at Cape Town in South Africa, for example. It is such a beautiful place! Yet as you arrive and from the airport, you are immediately faced by Khayelitsha, the biggest slum in the whole country. And what about Ajegunle in Lagos? Thousands of rickety shacks vying for space. It is the same in Kenya with the Kibera and Mathare slums which are virtual "no go areas" in the heart of Nairobi. Abidjan's informal settlements come to my mind, of course. Or Mexico City for that matter, with its slums which must have one of the highest levels of pollution in the world. I am also thinking of many Black neighborhoods in the US. Poverty has no borders. The examples are limitless. The image of birds (as opposed to bats) is one of hope. Hope that cities can be rebuilt on a human scale.

JAM: I see that you make reference to several African countries and even to countries outside the continent. For whom is *The Blind Kingdom* intended ... did you have a particular audience in mind? *The Blind Kingdom* requires, or at the very least, calls for a particular kind of literacy, don't you think –VèVè Clark named this "Diaspora Literacy."

VT: It is always a difficult question to answer. You don't write for a whole country or for the whole world. You wouldn't be able to put down a line! On the contrary, you must try to avoid outside contingencies that might divert you from what you are trying to say. There is a story in you and you have to work hard at bringing it out. But the challenge is that it has to be rooted in the particular, while at the same time, have the potential to become relevant to other people outside this reality. So, in this sense I can say that I had an African audience or even to be more precise an Ivorian audience in mind. Yet, my main interest was to produce a story about some human beings' struggle to create a better world.

JAM: This book was published in 1990 ... yet it resonates loudly with the political scene in Côte d'Ivoire since 2002 ... the Grand North, the South ... rebels and up-risings. Of your novels, this one and *The Shadow of Imana*, about the 1994 genocide in Rwanda get to the heart of violence and creativity ... beautiful things can come from violence and does violence necessarily stifle creativity?

VT: Let me take your question from the other end. I am fascinated by beauty. What is its function? Can it help us be better people? If you live in magnificent surroundings will you be more tolerant, less inclined to fight? Not necessarily. It cannot prevent violence or cruelty. Look at Rwanda. They call it, "the country of a thousand hills". It has a breathtaking country-side. Look at America. When the Red Indians were slaughtered, it was a virgin country full of forests, lakes and wonderful valleys. Through creativity, you attempt to put some order into the chaos. You look beyond the destruction to let life in again. You reaffirm our humanity. And may be the beauty you are talking about comes from this endeavor.

JAM: The Mask is often seen in ceremonies that takes place almost all over Africa. I want to explore this idea of ritual and spirituality. Which Mask are you talking about?

VT: I was thinking of a Mask from the Poro, the traditional religion of the Senoufo people from the North of Côte d'Ivoire. It is a very complex set of beliefs and rites which has mythical figures and a pantheon of gods. There are all sorts of Masks, virtually for every occasion. But the Mask which appears in the story is sacred and is a symbol of spirituality and creativity. It is highly charged with a significance and power that the elders have bestowed on it. The Poro have initiation rites and Akissi goes through some kind of an initiation herself. She evolves into a more conscious person able to see what is happening around herself.

JAM: This narrative reminds me of innovative creative work done by Black women writers such as Toni Morrison, Monifa Love, where the eye remains focused on the community ... the life within the community that can be traced back to moments, places and histories.

VT: Yes, in *The Blind kingdom,* I wanted to give a sense of community. I have read Morrison's writing and what I like about her novels is the fact that as a reader you can feel the vibrancy of the community. *The community is the main character.* It informs all the other protagonists' actions. Morrison's immense achievement is that she looks at her society with eyes wide open, scrutinizing every detail, good or bad. But the final image is one of resilience and love.

JAM: *The Blind Kingdom* is layered ... one image, one story on top of the other, some narratives jutting out, some short, some more vivid than others... Here I see a link between the visual and the literal, too. Why did you choose this particular style?

VT: I have been writing like this ever since my first book. I want to look at life from many different angles, so I use whatever is at my disposal as a writer and as an artist. We live in a community and in trying to tell one story in particular, I have to rely on other stories. Our destinies cross, we meet people, they enter our lives, then exit, to be replaced by others, etc. Our existence is layered by an amazing number of stories. So that's why I move in and out. Having done some photography, I am keenly aware of the danger of the focused picture. The viewer cannot see everything that happens around the subject while the photo is being taken. Literature in this sense offers more possibilities.

Moreover, I wanted the story to have a timeless dimension, especially because I thought that it was very topical. I therefore chose a form that would counter-balance the immediacy of the narrative. Tales are at the same time – ancestral and contemporary. It is all in the way you tell them, re-contextualize them. It is also a literary genre that is known to all cultures and which in a way touches all age groups. When they hear a tale, the listeners can understand it on many different levels, depending on their maturity and grasp of the cultural, historical or political references. But whatever the case they always get something from it. With time and added knowledge they can discover and unlock different keys in the narrative. As a writer, what attracts me to the tale is its freedom of expression. Virtually everything is allowed, even the mixture of genres (poetry, political speech, incantations, etc).

JAM: Artists often live in places like France, US and the UK. I read an interview where you were asked about being a writer in exile because you don't live in your country at the moment. Do you see yourself as a writer living in exile?

VT: Most of my life has been spent on the African continent but with lots of traveling abroad. When we talk of exile, I guess we talk of nationhood. And I guess that not having lived in Côte d'Ivoire on a permanent basis for a number of years now, makes me some kind of exile. But of course, that is forgetting that I am a Pan-Africanist at heart and as long as I am on the continent, I consider myself at home. And as long as I have free access to my country, I am fine.

JAM: By a 'Pan-Africanist at heart' what do you mean? Is there a politics involved or a knowing and feeling of kinship based on shared histories across the African world?

VT: It is important for me to constantly increase my knowledge of Africa. Living in different countries and traveling through the continent is invaluable. I am also interested in the Diaspora.

JAM: How have you connected the visual arts in general and painting in particular to your writing?

VT: Living with a mother who was an artist, a painter and a sculptor showed me that visual art was a very powerful way of expressing oneself. I understood with time that I did not need to feel torn between painting and illustrating and my writing. The most important thing was being in the process of creation. Whether you are a musician, a sculptor or a writer, what counts is creativity. You must choose the medium that best suits your objective at a given moment in your life. Painting came when I was in Kenya. The light there has a magnificent quality and there is a great community of artists. I was able to spend time with them and develop as a self-taught painter. I believe I am a better writer when I can also paint because it is about a different way of saying things, using different kinds of signs but in the end trying to tell a story.

JAM: What comparisons can one draw between then and now? Does *The Blind Kingdom* contain some predictions that have come true regarding your country?

VT: The parallel between the story and the present situation in Côte d'Ivoire is the South/North divide. The rebellion which took place in September 2002 marked the beginning of a deep political and military crisis. It was waged by rebels coming from the North of the country. They took control of key northern cities (Korhogo and Bouaké), effectively dividing the country into two. After many Peace Agreements and Accords, the line of demarcation has been dismantled. Côte d'Ivoire has regained a level of peace but it is yet to achieve lasting stability. It is important that as a people, we recognize that our cultural diversity is a source of richness. We must work harder at strengthening the concept of nationhood by looking at the country as an economic and social entity.

February 2008

Historical background to *The Blind Kingdom*

An interview conducted by Germain A. Kadi, Lecturer at the University of Bouaké, Côte d'Ivoire in 2006.

GAK: Can you tell me precisely when you wrote *The Blind Kingdom*?

VT: If I remember well, I wrote *The Blind Kingdom* between 1986 and 1990. I started it in Lagos and completed it in Paris. While I was in Lagos I was still attached to the University of Abidjan, giving semester courses. I did not stay long in Paris.

GAK: In 1990 when you went back to Côte d'Ivoire you taught at the university. Were you a member of the University staff union?

VT: Yes, I was a member of the Synares. But I can't say that I was a particularly fervent militant. I went to the union meetings, took part in the debates and followed the strike calls as much as possible. But I was never part of the leadership.

GAK: How did you personally experience the 1990 social crisis?

VT: 1990 was a very heated year. It was characterized by constant debating and we had the feeling that history was in the making. We had the impression that the country's destiny was being played out before our eyes. But at the same time, as far as I am concerned, there was a definite frustration because we were aware that Houphouët-Boigny's grasp on the country was weakening and that he wasn't in control of the political situation anymore. Moreover, apart from the struggle that the opposition was waging, it was obvious that external pressures were at work in his decision to relent to the introduction of the multi-party system. So we were faced with a politically weakened leader in a country that was in the midst of a severe economic crisis. Challenging him was an opponent (Laurent Gbagbo, the current president) who was riding on the wearing effect of power and the great desire for change which could be felt in the country and elsewhere in the world.

GAK: Are there not some similarities between President Houphouët-Boigny's life and Ato IV?

VT: Absolutely. In the characterization of Ato IV, I was greatly inspired by some aspects of Houphouët's figure as a political man. In my mind, our former (and first) president acted like a true Akan King all through his time in power up to his death. For example, he refused to name a credible successor arguing that according to tradition, "You don't talk about the king's death in his presence." There were also all sorts of myths surrounding him. Having been at the forefront of independence, he behaved as if he owned the country. I came to the conclusion that all his life he had ruled over a kingdom and that the members of the elite were totally blind to social injustices. They kept on living in luxury while the economic crisis was in full-swing. I thought that this was totally irresponsible and I could see that in the short or long term this could lead to a popular uprising if things continued in the same vein. I had lived for two years in the North of Côte d'Ivoire, so I was particularly conscious of the huge economic contrasts that existed between the North and the South as well as the political tensions that were brewing as a result of this situation.

I chose to call the king in *The Blind Kingdom*, Ato IV (a name from the East of Côte d'Ivoire), because I wanted to show that it was the nature of absolute power that leads to violence and rebellion and not the "ethnic" origin *per se* of the ruler.

This Interview was conducted for his research
on Ivorian Literature.

(Publisher's Note: This publication has been set
in American English to preserve the voice of the
Translator who is African American).